GRIEVING TOGETHER

A Couple's Journey through Miscarriage

Laura Kelly Fanucci
and Franco David Fanucci

Our Sunday Visitor

www.osv.com
Our Sunday Visitor Publishing Division
Our Sunday Visitor, Inc.
Huntington, Indiana 46750

Nihil Obstat:
Msgr. Michael Heintz, Ph.D.
Censor Librorum

Imprimatur:
✠ Kevin C. Rhoades
Bishop of Fort Wayne-South Bend
July 17, 2018

The *Nihil Obstat* and *Imprimatur* are declarations that a work is free from doctrinal or moral error. It is not implied that those who have granted the *Nihil Obstat* and *Imprimatur* agree with the contents, opinions, or statements expressed.

For the one we never got to hold.

CONTENTS

mind us that miscarriage is understood by millions, even if our culture doesn't often speak of it or acknowledge our children.

We wrote this book to let you know you are not alone. We wanted to reach out to mothers and fathers who are reeling from grief and wondering how to move forward after their hopes have been shattered. We have been where you are today, and we wished then that we had a guide through grief. While everyone experiences loss differently, there are common questions, concerns, and challenges we often share. Learning from each other is a way that God can call us to journey through grief together.

The loss of a baby is at once a common suffering and a deeply personal loss. People try to normalize it with statistics or share stories of others who have had miscarriages, but you are the only one who lost this particular child, a unique and unrepeatable soul. Your pain cannot be minimized. Your grief springs from your love as a parent.

This book is unique because it speaks to the particular experiences of both mother and father after the death of a baby. Fathers are often forgotten in the aftermath of miscarriage, but they, too, have suffered the loss of a child. Through chapters written specifically for mothers and fathers, we provide practical resources for both women and men. We hope that all parents will feel welcome within these pages.

The idea of grieving together does not mean grieving in perfect unison. It means trying to keep your marriage at the center of your life, even on grief's hardest days. You do not have to read this book with your spouse, although it can provide perspective on how they may be feeling or acting. Our approach does not aim to make anyone work through grief in a particular way. Grief has no instruction manual. But this book can be a companion on the journey: it is a collection of perspectives, prayers, resources, and Scripture to let you know that no matter your experience, God is with you in your pain.

To help you journey through grief together, we share personal stories from numerous couples who have experienced miscarriage. We also offer reflection questions at the end of each chapter for personal journaling or conversation starters as a couple. While men and women often grieve differently, miscarriage does not have to drive us apart. We can learn to communicate through our complicated, changing emotions and even grow closer together as we seek to move forward in faith.

This book draws from Catholic tradition and teaching, with the hope that all who have experienced miscarriage can find help within these pages. Questions of "Why did God let this happen?" and "Was this God's plan?" naturally arise after loss, so we will explore the wisdom of the Church on suffering, death, and salvation. We also gather Scripture, saints, prayers, and rites that offer grieving couples the Church's compassion and comfort.

While miscarriage is our focus, this book can also speak to parents who have experienced stillbirth or infant loss. Since we as authors have experienced the death of babies after birth, we hold all this grief together in our writing when we use the language of miscarriage. This book does not include discussion of abortion, but it is equally important to grieve this deep loss and seek healing. Especially if you have had an abortion in the past and then experience a miscarriage, your grief may resurface in ways that can benefit from professional support beyond the scope of this resource. (Information on Project Rachel, the Catholic Church's ministry for post-abortion healing, can be found at hopeafterabortion.com.)

You can use this book in whatever way you need. You may wish to read it alone or share part of it with your spouse. Depending on how recently you suffered your miscarriage, you may wish to read the book straight through or skip ahead to a chapter that speaks to you today.

- **Part I** — The Experience of Miscarriage (Chapters 1–2) — describes the physical and emotional experience of miscarriage, including practical decisions about medical treatment and funeral/burial options for your child.
- **Part II** — How Couples Respond to Grief (Chapters 3–6) — explores particular aspects of grieving as a mother, father, and couple, to help you understand why you and your spouse may grieve differently and how you can support each other.
- **Part III** — Family, Friends, and the Church (Chapters 7–9) — gathers practical suggestions for how loved ones can sup-

port you, theological teaching on suffering and salvation, and pastoral resources that speak to miscarriage (including Scripture, sacraments, saints, prayers, and official Church rites).

- **Part IV** — The Future after Miscarriage (Chapters 10–12) — offers ideas for honoring your child's memory, ways to strengthen your marriage through loss, and perspectives on what might come next for you as a couple, whether you conceive again or do not go on to have more children.

This book can also be a helpful resource for pastors, parish ministers, marriage mentor couples, doctors, nurses, hospital staff, chaplains, counselors, friends, and families — all who prepare couples for the realities of married life, support couples trying to conceive, or minister to grieving parents. In Catholic tradition, "to bury the dead" is a corporal work of mercy; "to comfort the sorrowful" and "to pray for the living and the dead" are spiritual works of mercy. The more we can grow as a Church in our pastoral care for couples who experience miscarriage, the more we can carry out the call of the Gospel to love our neighbor and to care for those who mourn.

As authors, we are not medical professionals or grief counselors. We are fellow travelers on the road: parents who have suffered significant losses yet have grown in our marriage because of the gifts of our children's lives. To answer the invitation to write this book out of our own grief was a true calling, because we have learned over the years how powerful it is to share stories of brokenness and heartache. We are grateful for all the parents who have shared their stories of love and loss with us over the years, and we are deeply indebted to those whose stories are gathered within the book you hold in your hands.

No single book can cover everyone's needs or circumstances. We drew from real experiences of couples to speak to a variety of situations. But just as miscarriage happens under different circumstances, so is grief experienced uniquely. We hope that you will take what resonates with you from this book and that it may point you toward other helpful resources (gathered in the Appendices). Above all, we pray that you will know you are not alone in your suffering and grief. As we wrote this book, we prayed for you — that each reader might find a word of comfort in God's love.

"It wasn't supposed to be like this." This refrain went through our heads a thousand times after our own miscarriage. We imagine you might have felt the same. None of us wanted or expected to be here. But since we are here together, let us draw closer — in our marriages, our families, and our communities of faith — to support each other in grief and in hope.

We wrote this book to remind parents that God remains close to us no matter what happens. We believe that even though the loss of a child brings deep heartache, God can still work powerfully to bring about healing and transformation in our lives. Our doubts, questions, anger, confusion, envy, sorrow, and struggles are nothing to hide, for the Lord is close to the brokenhearted.

The lament of our lives is a holy prayer to God, who loves us. Our God who heard the cries of his beloved son from the cross knows what it means to lose a child, too. The compassion of God's own heart will carry us from the agony of the cross to the promise of the empty tomb. May the God of infinite mercy hold you in your sorrow and lead you into fullness of life — the joy of the resurrection, when you will be reunited with your beloved child forever.

> Just as you do not know how the life breath
>   enters the human frame in the mother's womb,
> So you do not know the work of God,
>   who is working in everything. (Eccl 11:5)

Part I

The Experience of Miscarriage

CHAPTER 1

When Miscarriage Happens

*In his hand is the soul of every living thing,
and the life breath of all mortal flesh. (Jb 12:10)*

W hen miscarriage happens, it can be overwhelming. This chapter helps you to navigate the physical process, common questions, and practical concerns surrounding the loss of a baby. Understanding the physical and medical aspects of miscarriage is an important first step before attending to the emotional and spiritual aspects of grief. The initial experiences and decisions surrounding miscarriage can be challenging or overwhelming. As a couple, you can help each other through these difficult experiences by communicating with each other, discussing any questions or concerns with your health care providers, and praying for the strength to support each other.

This chapter is organized by common questions that couples often ask in the immediate hours, days, and weeks surrounding miscarriage. Please note that the information provided here is not intended to replace the expertise of a trained medical professional. Contact your OB/GYN, midwife, or family physician with any concerns or questions regarding your physical and mental health.

What is miscarriage?

Miscarriage is generally defined as the loss of a baby in pregnancy before twenty weeks gestation. One in four pregnancies end in miscarriage, most often due to chromosomal abnormalities that produce a damaged sperm or egg cell or due to a problem that occurred during an early stage of the baby's development. Miscarriages can also be caused by hormonal issues, infections, maternal health issues (including maternal age or trauma), or other issues (for example, if the fertilized egg does not implant properly into the lining of the uterus).

Up to 75 percent of miscarriages occur within the first twelve weeks of pregnancy. Common symptoms are vaginal bleeding (usually brown spotting that turns red) and abdominal cramping. However, many women experience vaginal bleeding during pregnancy and do not miscarry, so it is important to seek professional medical help if you suspect a miscarriage.

The term "miscarriage" can refer to many different situations in which a baby dies before birth. Knowing the terminology can help you understand your particular situation. It is also important to know that the medical terms surrounding miscarriage may be difficult for you to hear. **Spontaneous abortion** is the technical term for a miscarriage, which can be an upsetting or emotional word for a woman to see in her medical files. Medical professionals will often refer to the baby as the "fetus" or "products of conception," or will use the term "fetal demise" to describe the death of a baby in the uterus. While many doctors and nurses are compassionate in understanding how difficult these terms can be for parents, you can also advocate for yourself and your child by continuing to refer to your "baby" and asking your health care providers to do the same.

It is also possible to have no symptoms and to learn of a miscarriage from a routine ultrasound. This is called a **missed miscarriage** and may or may not be signaled by a loss of pregnancy symptoms like morning sickness or breast tenderness. In a missed miscarriage, the baby has died but the actual miscarriage has not yet begun.

A **spontaneous miscarriage** happens on its own, without medical intervention. In an **incomplete miscarriage** the baby has died but everything in the uterus has not been expelled. In this case, medical intervention is usually necessary to empty the uterus (of the placenta, for example) and avoid the risk of infection or hemorrhage.

Early miscarriages are often caused by a chemical pregnancy or blighted ovum. In a **chemical pregnancy**, the pregnancy is confirmed by a blood test or home pregnancy test but is not yet visible by ultrasound. The miscarriage occurs shortly after implantation, resulting in bleeding close to the time of the woman's expected menstrual period. Chemical pregnancies may be the cause of 50–75 percent of all miscarriages. A **blighted ovum** happens when a fertilized egg implants into the uterine wall but does not develop. An ultrasound may show a gestational sac with or without a yolk sac, but the baby does not grow.

> *"You can also advocate for yourself and your child by continuing to refer to your 'baby' and asking your health care providers to do the same."*

Vanishing twin syndrome is another kind of miscarriage, in which a twin (or multiple) is miscarried and absorbed by the remaining baby, the placenta, or the uterus. Vanishing twin syndrome usually happens early in the first trimester and is estimated to occur in 20–30 percent of multiple pregnancies — now detected more frequently because of the use of early ultrasounds.

Ectopic or tubal pregnancy happens when a fertilized egg implants elsewhere than the uterus, most commonly in the fallopian tube. This is almost always fatal for the baby and can cause serious complications or death for the mother. If the tube ruptures, the mother will not only experience great pain but may have so much bleeding that she goes into shock.

In a **molar pregnancy**, there is an abnormal combination of sperm and egg. Instead of a sperm and an egg uniting, sometimes an "empty egg" is fertilized by two sperm, resulting in a **complete molar pregnancy** (with only genetic material from the father and none of the mother's chromosomes). Sometimes the egg will have normal genetic make-up and will be fertilized by two sperm, resulting in a **partial molar pregnancy**. In both of these conditions, the tissues that grow and develop are similar to the tissue that ordinarily makes up the placenta. In a partial molar pregnancy, there may be a baby along with the abnormal tissue, but the baby is unable to survive. All molar pregnancies end in miscarriage, so both conditions require a procedure to remove this tissue from the uterus. In some rare cases, molar pregnancy can lead to a unique form of uterine cancer, and therefore doctors generally recommend that women avoid getting pregnant again for six to twelve months, until pregnancy hormone levels (HCG) go back to zero.

A **threatened miscarriage** involves vaginal bleeding without cervical dilation that may lead to miscarriage before twenty weeks gestation. In the case of threatened miscarriage, a doctor or midwife may recommend bed rest or extra monitoring. **Recurrent miscarriages** are commonly defined as three or more consecutive first-trimester miscarriages. If you have experienced multiple losses, your doctor will likely recommend further blood work and testing to determine possible causes.

Stillbirth is defined as the death of a baby before birth, after twenty weeks gestation. The baby must still be delivered, either by cesarean section or vaginal birth. **Preterm delivery** is the live birth of a baby between twenty and thirty-seven weeks, even before the point of fetal viability at which a baby can survive outside the womb (generally accepted to be between twenty-two and twenty-four weeks). An **adverse prenatal diagnosis** is when the unborn child is diagnosed with a serious medical condition that may be "incompatible with life" after birth.

What does miscarriage feel like?

Miscarriages can happen under a variety of circumstances. Some miscarriages happen suddenly and without warning; others can take weeks to occur. Active miscarriage can feel as intense as labor, or the pain may be relatively mild. It can take a few days or a few hours. This range of physical experiences does not necessarily correspond to how long you have been pregnant. (Many women who have an early miscarriage are surprised to find that it feels like labor, especially since miscarriage is often mischaracterized as a heavy period.) Depending on how far along you are in your pregnancy, your doctor may advise inducing labor to deliver your baby.

Follow the recommendations of your doctor or midwife for your particular situation. Depending on the circumstances, you may have time to consider certain choices for medical or surgical treatment. Every option can have different risks, so it is important to discuss and weigh the emotional and physical impact of each. Spouses can talk through options together, pray over the choices, and make sure all your questions are answered by your health care professionals so that you can make a well-informed decision under difficult circumstances.

If you decide to "watch and wait," you can usually expect to miscarry naturally within two weeks after the baby has died. (See Appendix A for websites that provide a detailed description of the physical process.) Some women prefer to miscarry in the privacy and comfort of their own home. This natural process can allow you to experience delivery and see your baby, which some couples feel provides closure and the best chance of burying their child's remains. If you choose to miscarry at home, contact your doctor if you experience excessive bleeding, fever, or intense pain, as these can be signs of complication. If you haven't miscarried after two weeks, you will need to contact your health care provider, since the risk of infection and blood clots increases the longer you wait to miscarry naturally.

Other women are overwhelmed by the prospect of miscarrying naturally, so they choose medical management. Misoprostol is the medicine most commonly administered by a doctor to help the uterus contract and expel any remaining contents, usually within one or two days. Generally, this process still allows you to miscarry at home, unless it is after the first trimester (or after eight weeks, depending on your doctor), in which case you will need to go to the hospital. Medical management of miscarriage can be quicker than waiting to miscarry naturally, which is emotionally preferable to some couples.

If your body does not pass the baby and tissue completely, you may need to undergo a surgical procedure called dilation and curettage (known as a D&C) or a dilation and evacuation (or D&E). Provided that your doctor has confirmed the baby's death by ultrasound prior to the procedure, it is morally permissible to empty the uterus surgically (usually done by vacuum evacuation). Generally, you will have the option to choose either local or general anesthesia. This outpatient procedure is the quickest way to manage a miscarriage and usually provides the quickest recovery. You can expect mild cramping for one to two days and light bleeding for about a week. However, you will not have an intact body to bury, although you can still request the remains for burial.

For an ectopic pregnancy, you will need to consult with your doctor about how to proceed in terms of surgery, since the baby cannot survive outside the uterus. (See Appendix A for more information on surgical options for ectopic pregnancy from the National Catholic Bioethics Center.) A ruptured ectopic pregnancy is a medical emergency and can be fatal for the mother if untreated, so you will need to have surgery immediately (usually a laparoscopic surgery performed with a camera through a small incision).

How can I prepare for miscarriage?

It is impossible to prepare fully for everything that miscarriage will bring, physically or emotionally. But if you have learned of the death of your baby and are waiting to miscarry, you will likely have time to prepare for the passing of your baby by taking time to make decisions with your spouse. During this time, you can also pray to God for emotional and spiritual strength as well as physical healing.

Depending on your circumstances (e.g., an adverse prenatal diagnosis), you may wish to consider creating a "birth plan" to approach the day of delivery. Here are some guidelines for preparing your plan:

- Contact a local bereavement doula who is trained to provide physical, emotional, and informational support to couples facing the loss of a baby.
- Ask to meet with a priest or hospital chaplain to pray together before or after your surgery or delivery. Refer to the official Church rites in Chapter 9 and Appendix C for specific prayers that may be used to bless you and your child.
- In terms of caring for your baby's body and preparing for burial, inquire whether any recommended chromosomal testing can be performed from the placenta or umbilical cord instead of the baby's body itself.
- Discuss seeing your baby. Parents are often anxious beforehand, but nurses and other medical personnel can help explain what your baby may look like. Many parents report being grateful that they decided to see and hold their baby, since this time together is precious.
- Plan to spend time with your baby. You may wish to hold your baby, wrap him or her in a blanket (which you can then keep), read or sing to your baby. You may decide to invite family members to meet, hold, and say their goodbyes to the baby, including grandparents or siblings.
- Consider taking pictures of your baby. Parents sometimes regret not taking pictures while they had the chance. You may wish to ask the nurses to take photos of your baby, and you can decide later if you want to see them. Now I Lay Me Down To Sleep is an organization of professional-quality photographers who will take free remembrance photos, generally for babies twenty-two weeks or older. (Find a photographer online at nowilaymedowntosleep.org).
- Collect keepsakes for a baby book or memory box such as baby hats, blankets, hospital bracelets, footprints and handprints, or clay imprints of hands and feet. "Angel gown" ministries across the country turn wedding dresses into free gowns or wraps for babies who died during pregnancy or after birth. These gowns can be worn in the hospital, for photos, or for burial.

How can I collect my child's remains?

If you choose to deliver at home, you may have time to obtain a miscarriage kit to collect the remains. (See Appendix A for where to order a kit.) These kits commonly include a plastic colander to catch the remains, a squirt bottle to wash the remains, a plastic bag for storage of the placenta, a vessel in which to place the baby with saline water, and rubber gloves. You may wish to find a photo of a baby at the same gestational age as your child to know what to expect, but please be warned that such photos can often be difficult to see. Afterward you should store the container with saline water in the refrigerator to slow decomposition of the body while you prepare for burial.

If you miscarry at the hospital or have a D&C, you may need to advocate for yourself and your child in order to obtain the remains of your baby's body. Medical personnel may dismiss this request by using a technical term like "products of conception" or telling you there is "nothing there." While local laws that govern the care of such remains require research as they vary from state to state, you can educate yourself on your rights as a patient and a parent. (For a helpful list of your rights during miscarriage, see Appendix A.)

What can I expect for physical recovery after miscarriage?

Bleeding usually lasts for two weeks and may be heavier than your normal period, although it should taper off by the end. Most women get their period again within four to six weeks, although your cycles may be irregular for several months. If you miscarry spontaneously, the doctor will typically do a follow-up ultrasound or exam to make sure your uterus is now empty. If you experience chills, fever, severe abdominal pain, foul-smelling discharge, or an increase in bleeding, contact your physician immediately, as these can be signs of complication or infection.

What can I do when my milk comes in?

If you have experienced a second-trimester miscarriage, stillbirth, or infant loss, your milk will likely come in shortly after birth. (Milk can come in with an early miscarriage as well, but it is more likely the further along you were in your pregnancy.) This can be a painful emotional and physical experience. Some mothers choose to pump their milk and donate to a milk bank for use in a local NICU. This gift of self can be a beautiful way to honor the memory of your child and help other babies in need. But it is not a decision that works for everyone. Many mothers want their milk to dry up as quickly as possible. However, small amounts of milk may be present in your breasts for weeks or even months after the miscarriage. Initial engorgement should pass in a few days. If you are not finding relief, consult your doctor on whether you should hand-express or pump milk.

To dry up your milk, try the following suggestions:

- Avoid stimulating your nipples.
- Use ice packs or cold compresses to relieve pain.
- Take a pain reliever like ibuprofen or acetaminophen.
- Wear a tight sports bra, even while sleeping.
- Use cold cabbage leaves for engorgement.
- Take a hot shower or bath to help your milk let down and relieve pressure if needed.

When can we try to conceive again?

Many couples are able to start trying to conceive in the first cycle after miscarriage. But you should consult with your health care provider for advice on your particular situation. If you have had three consecutive miscarriages, your doctor will likely recommend testing to investigate an underlying problem like uterine abnormalities, blood disorders, abnormal hormone levels, infection, fibroids, or an incompetent cervix (a condition when the cervix opens before full-term). You may also wish to consult with a doctor trained in Na-Pro Technology (which stands for Natural Procreative Technology, a women's health science which offers treatments for infertility and recurrent miscarriage based on the Creighton Model of Natural Family Planning).

Statistically, the majority of couples are able to conceive again after miscarriage and carry a pregnancy to term. Recent studies have even suggested that trying to conceive within the first three months after miscarriage may be more likely to result in a pregnancy. But the prospect of another pregnancy can be a complicated and emotional decision that invites careful consideration and prayerful discernment. (For more about pregnancy after loss, see Chapter 12.)

Understanding the physical process of miscarriage and your medical options for treatment is important for healing and healthy grieving. As a patient and a parent, you have the right to know what is happening and to make decisions informed by your faith and the guidance of trusted medical professionals. As spouses, you can seek to support each other as best you can, leaning on the mercy and wisdom of God's compassionate love for you and your child.

REFLECTION QUESTIONS

What has been the hardest part of your experience surrounding miscarriage?

What kind of support do you need right now?

Alex's story

When my wife started to bleed, she called me at work. I left work as quickly and discreetly as I could to meet her at the doctor's office. A quick ultrasound revealed no heartbeat. Our first baby, who would have been eleven weeks gestation, had died. I felt like this couldn't be real. This was not what was supposed to happen. As we left the doctor's office, we both knew we couldn't go back to work. So we picked up some takeout and went home to comfort each other as best we could.

At that time, miscarriage was not something any of our friends had experienced — just like the several months of infertility we experienced before and after losing our baby. Everyone around us was announcing new pregnancies. It was difficult not to distort the news of friends we love and support into a personal insult. We were hurting, and instead of feeling able to share our infertility and miscarriage with those around us, babies became a topic to dance around delicately in conversation to avoid the dreaded question: "When do you think you'll have kids?"

The day we found out our baby had died, my mom came over to see how we were doing. She gave me a hug and said, "I'm so, so sorry."

"It's ok" was my automatic response.

"No, it's not," she told me with tears in her eyes, "but it will be." It was then that I remembered that my mom had two miscarriages many years before. Sharing that connection with someone else who had experienced what we were going through was a first step toward healing.

In the years since our miscarriage, we've seen friends go through the same experience. It has made me grieve that we didn't feel we could be more open with the loss of our child while it was happening. But the healing that we have experienced has given me opportunities to be the presence to others that I wish we had years ago. We will never forget the baby that we never had the chance to meet, and there are holes in our hearts that will not be filled on this earth.

The solution that God gives for this pain is not the same for everyone. For us, it was to have two more children, and God willing, several more in the future. For those who will not be blessed in this way, they will surely be a blessing to others through the witness of their experience and will share the graces of parenthood with those around them in whatever way God has planned.

Anna's story

No one ever told me what it would be like to miscarry a baby. No one told me that I would still experience the pain of contractions, or that I would feel my dead baby pass out of me, or that I would bleed for weeks afterward, a constant reminder of what I had lost. No one told me that people might say insensitive things to me, like "at that stage, it wasn't really a baby yet" or "I felt left out of your life when you were pregnant." No one told me that losing a baby would change me forever.

We never named the baby we lost. I never felt moved to do so, until almost a year after we miscarried. It was Holy Week, and we were singing in the choir at our parish's Easter Vigil. It was the part of the liturgy where we sang the long Easter version of the Litany of the Saints. I was beginning to zone out a little bit when I heard "Saint Anastasia, pray for us." And I started to weep. There was no way for me to know if the baby we lost was a boy or a girl. But as I heard the name Anastasia, I knew that was what we should name our baby. I knew that that soul which I had carried for such a short time was in heaven with all the saints, before the throne of God, praying for me.

It would be two more years before I carried a baby to term. They were the hardest years of my life. But they were also years of incredible growth, both in my marriage and in my relationship with God. My husband and I were united in our grief and in our desire for a child. We were also united in seeking God's will for our marriage, praying that it included children, and trusting that if it didn't, He would give us the grace to accept His plan.

CHAPTER 2

After Miscarriage

"I do not know how you came to be in my womb; it was not I who gave you breath and life, nor was it I who arranged the elements you are made of. Therefore, since it is the Creator of the universe who shaped the beginning of humankind and brought about the origin of everything, he, in his mercy, will give you back both breath and life." (2 Mc 7:22–23)

The immediate aftermath of miscarriage can be one of the hardest times in grief, both physically and emotionally. This chapter addresses practical and spiritual questions that arise right after miscarriage, including how to care for your child and how to navigate initial struggles as newly bereaved parents.

Can we baptize our baby?
If your baby is born alive, he or she may be baptized immediately. The Catholic Church clearly states that "an infant in danger of death

is to be baptized without delay" (Canon 867.2). Furthermore, in the event of such an emergency, anyone can baptize: "In imminent danger of death and especially at the moment of death, when no priest or deacon is available, any member of the faithful, indeed anyone with the right intention, may and sometimes must administer baptism."[1] In the case of emergency, all that is necessary for a lay person to do (who has the intention to do what the Church does while baptizing) is to pour water three times over the baby's head while pronouncing the baptismal formula; "N., I baptize you in the name of the Father, and of the Son, and of the Holy Spirit."

The Catholic Church does not baptize those who have died. So if the baby has already died (as in miscarriage or stillbirth), you do not need to baptize. Sacraments are for the living, and the souls of the dead are already in the all-loving and merciful hands of God. There are still official rites and blessings that can be offered for your baby after miscarriage or stillbirth, however. (See chapter 8 for further explanation of the Church's teaching on baptism and chapter 9 for rites that can be performed by a priest or deacon.)

Can we name our baby?

Naming your baby is a beautiful way to express your love for your child. If you miscarried early in the pregnancy or did not learn the gender of your baby, you can pick a gender-neutral name. Some couples choose one male and one female name to create a first and middle name combination like Maria Joseph or Francis Grace. You could also find inspiration from a saint's name from the feast of the day that you found out you were pregnant or the day your baby died. If you did not name your child immediately after the miscarriage, you can return to this idea months or even years later — as a way to care for your child and honor their memory.

Can we bury our baby?

Some couples find caring for their baby's remains to be a healing part of grieving. Others are unaware that this was an option they could have considered. If you miscarried at home, the baby's remains may have been flushed down the toilet. If you miscarried in the hospital,

---

1. *Rite of Baptism for Children*, no. 16.

the remains may have been disposed of by the hospital staff. If either of these scenarios were the case, please do not burden yourself with guilt over the past. As the *Catechism of the Catholic Church* reminds us, we entrust our beloved children to the abundant mercy of God (CCC 1261).

If you were able to keep the remains of your baby, you can find local options for burying the remains. You may first need to research your state's laws about obtaining and transporting your child's remains from the hospital or doctor's office. Some Catholic hospitals offer committal and burial services several times a year for miscarried and stillborn babies. Local funeral homes may also have memorial services for miscarried babies. You may be able to find assistance for funeral funds through local Catholic organizations or groups dedicated to pregnancy and infant loss. For example, the monks at New Melleray Abbey offer infant caskets at no cost to families who have lost a child. (See Appendix A for contact information.)

You will also need to research cemeteries in your area to learn about your options. Some cemeteries have special areas set aside for babies; others may allow you to bury a miscarried baby on a family member's grave. Certain cemeteries offer discounted fees or free burials for babies, while others charge the same amount as for an adult burial. If you buy a gravesite for your baby, there is generally a price for the plot as well as a fee to open and close the grave. You can inquire with cemetery officials about what local monument companies are typically used for gravestones and what size marker is allowed. You may also be able to use an online monument company or have your child's name engraved on the back of a shared monument, if your child is buried in a common area with other miscarried babies.

The Catholic Church offers Funeral Rites for Children, including particular prayers for children who died before baptism. These rites include options for a vigil, funeral within or outside of Mass, and the committal of the body (see chapter 9). Please note that not all pastors are familiar with how these rites may be used in case of miscarriage, so you may need to share these resources with your parish when you inquire about a funeral and/or burial for your baby. But the healing power of ritual and liturgy can speak to parents even years later who decide to have a memorial Mass celebrated for their child.

Can we have our baby cremated?

While the Church has not always allowed cremation, it is now an option permitted for Catholics (CCC 2301). The Church teaches that cremated remains should be buried in a cemetery or columbarium (a building or wall for the storage of funerary urns), rather than being scattered as ashes or kept at home. Burying your baby in a cemetery, columbarium, or mausoleum (a building with tombs, often located in a cemetery) allows the whole Christian community to join you in praying for your child. Burying the dead is a corporal work of mercy according to Catholic tradition, and this act of faith speaks to our belief in the resurrection, when the faithful will rise and receive glorified bodies in heaven.

What can we expect in the early days after miscarriage?

The first days and weeks may feel like a fog. Both spouses are in a state of shock, physically drained, and emotionally exhausted, yet the world expects you to carry on. You may be consumed by sorrow, anger, or guilt. You may find yourself needing extra sleep while still having little appetite. Returning to work, caring for other children, and having to interact with the "real world" can feel overwhelming and draining

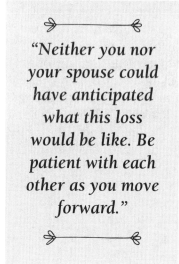

"Neither you nor your spouse could have anticipated what this loss would be like. Be patient with each other as you move forward."

Be gentle with yourself as you live in "survival mode" for the first few weeks at home, particularly in cooking, cleaning, or child care. Grief can feel surprisingly exhausting for both spouses, but especially for the mother who is recovering from the physical toll on her body (and may have restrictions in daily activities). While the husband can demonstrate his love and concern by taking on more of the household tasks and allowing his wife to rest, it is also a moment to allow others to help you both. Take people up on their offers to bring food, run errands, watch your children, or clean the house. The intensity of early grief will not last forever, and gradually you will both regain the energy to resume your regular routines little by little.

Telling family and friends, whether or not you had shared the news of your pregnancy before, can be emotional and difficult. You may wish to ask someone to be your "spokesperson" and convey the news outside your immediate circle so that you are not exhausted by retelling the story over and over. (See chapter 6 for suggestions on how to talk to children about miscarriage.)

Once the initial shock wears off, you may find that you need more support. One source of immediate help can be medical professionals, starting with the doctors, midwives, nurses, or doulas who cared for you during your pregnancy or miscarriage. You can also contact your hospital for a referral to local resources, including chaplains, grief counselors, therapists, or pregnancy loss support groups. Another source of support can be your pastor, parish ministers, or the local diocesan office of marriage and family. Some parishes offer a chapter of Elizabeth Ministry International or similar outreach to women and families. (See Appendix A for further information.)

No matter the decisions you make — in naming, blessing, or burying your baby, and in seeking out support for yourself — remember that you are doing the best you can under difficult circumstances. Neither you nor your spouse could have anticipated what this loss would be like. Be patient with each other as you move forward.

You may already feel that this loss has divided your life into "before" and "after." Indeed, you have entered into a new chapter of your life after miscarriage. Part II of this book (How Couples Respond to Grief) will help you to understand how each of you may be processing this loss differently — and how miscarriage might affect your marriage. Remember that even in the immediate aftermath of miscarriage, you are not alone. You are journeying through grief together. The road may be rocky; its twists and turns may lead you into unexpected or difficult terrain. But you are together, and God is with you.

What sources of support have helped you after miscarriage?

If you decided to name your baby, how did you choose the name?

Megan and Peter's story

It wasn't a good time for another baby. I was working long days in the military, with an eleven-month-old and two-year-old at home. Exhausted and filled with dread, I vowed not to tell anyone at work before it was necessary. Pregnancy was looked down upon in my profession because its restrictions interfered with training and certain duties. My only solace was the shining light in my husband's eyes. With the discovery of each new child, he had reminded me that it would be okay in the end.

I wrestled with the reality of this new life, telling myself I should be grateful. On the drive home from work I bared my soul to God, holding up my weakness and soaking up the reassurance He poured out in return: this life is also a gift. Those who will respond in judgment won't be part of my life forever. By the end of the drive my little *fiat* had taken root. The seed of hope was blossoming.

But when the alarm clock rang the next morning, I froze in terror. Something was wrong: I was bleeding. I shook my husband awake, and his eyes widened. Numbly, we pulled on our uniforms, and I decided to go to the military clinic. The nurses gave me a pregnancy test: positive. They sent me to the physician's assistant. "Don't cry," I ordered myself. "Whatever you do, don't cry." Against my will, silent tears started falling.

"Your cervix is dilated," she said quietly. "I'll get ibuprofen for the cramping." Somehow, I drove to my office, stony face firmly in place.

It was early in my pregnancy, and the cramping resembled a normal menstrual cycle. I knew nothing of options to collect remains or to ask a priest for assistance. I returned to work as usual. I vacillated between self-blame, frustration, and numbness. It was my fault because I hadn't wanted a baby right then. I'd caused it by exercising instead of telling my boss I was pregnant. Was my miscarriage nothing compared to friends whose losses were later, who had to grieve babies they could touch, see, and hold?

I ached not knowing whether my baby was a boy or girl. How could I love fully when I didn't know my baby fully? But deep down, my spirit whispered that Sovereign God, Author of Life, not only had His reasons, but in His infinite love He wept with me.

The pain still surfaced raw and deep. A month later during field training, I began lactating in response to the baby who was long gone. Blessedly, my boss who had experienced her own loss granted me permission to briefly leave and buy a pump so I could avoid infection. That night, I sat in a tent on a cot with my new hand pump and silently wept for my baby.

Slowly, acceptance came. A friend sent me Mother Angelica's miscarriage prayer, opening my eyes to the beauty of our personal intercessor in heaven. Eventually we chose a name for our baby. My husband gave me a pair of pearl earrings for our anniversary, the birthstone of the month our baby would have been due.

Whenever I mentioned my story, other women's voices joined the chorus, more than I'd ever realized. Each of their stories echoed the truth in my heart: a life existed, and a love was born. While death came first, love makes a space to carry the same eternal life in our hearts.

The miscarriage had shattered my carefully constructed reality and made me question my fertility. Though I briefly acknowledged my sadness, I told myself it was good that I wasn't too deeply affected and could continue "normal" life. I tried not to think too long about the baby we had lost and instead focused on the one we might have one day.

We talked about the future, baby names, rearranging bedrooms

— topics that kept us optimistic. When I arrived home from a month of training, my husband and I rejoiced at the timing for my chances of getting pregnant. A week later, the tell-tale nausea hit. I was clearly pregnant! But test after test came back negative. Within a week the nausea faded, and my cycle returned. I grieved over my clear symptoms that had not resulted in a baby. Two weeks later, my pain was worse than ever — but I thought it was my endometriosis. Then mid-cycle spotting started, which had never happened before.

It was almost midnight when I found myself driving to the ER, shaking like a leaf. Deep down I knew that something was wrong. In the ER, the pregnancy test came back positive. An ultrasound revealed an ectopic pregnancy. I had been right: I was pregnant, but now the baby I carried had no chance of survival. The pain of the first loss flooded me anew. I tried to wrap my head around the fact that my body once again was rejecting my baby — this time a baby we had hoped and prayed for. Why?

The memories come back in flashes. An IV of morphine, a nurse telling me sternly to calm down when the sobs and fear took over. Asking for a priest and being told that none were available. Trying to research licit treatment for an ectopic pregnancy on my phone. Deciding on emergency surgery and leaving the decision of whether to remove my tube or just the baby in the surgeon's hands.

After surgery I focused on physical recovery, my brain telling my heart that getting emotional and dwelling on the past wouldn't help. I found an article on ectopic pregnancy treatment from the National Catholic Bioethics Center, and after going to confession at least three times for what I felt was the wrong treatment, I delivered the article to my surgeon. I presented my cheery self at work and seldom gave in to the tears at home. I was thankful that I hadn't fallen into depression, but I thought this meant I should spend as little time as possible thinking about the children whom we'd lost.

I slowly realized that grieving didn't mean walking around defeated and gloomy. It meant that I should take time to acknowledge the loss and allow myself to experience the depth of my sadness instead of minimizing or running from my grief. Then I could honor the children I didn't have the chance to hold, but still had the chance to love, just as I love my other children. I was also able to open myself to sharing the burden of grief with my husband, recognizing how he as a father also grieves for his children. We named our second child and now pray for their intercession every night along with the children we are blessed to raise.

Not a day goes by when I do not think of them, especially with my physical scars. But in the midst of pain I thank God for the blessings of each child, here on earth and in His care. So many questions remain unanswered, but I know that God loves more fully and grieves more deeply, because He understands the infinite value of a single life.

The grace God has poured out to sustain us is more than we could have ever imagined. I've learned that my condition and the loss of our children are not punishments. Nor do they mean that God doesn't care. Instead, through this suffering God has let us share in His heart more deeply, drawing nearer to Him to experience the fullness of His great love.

Part II

How Couples Respond to Grief

CHAPTER 3

Our Story

"But we hold this treasure in earthen vessels, that the surpassing power may be of God and not from us. We are afflicted in every way, but not constrained; perplexed, but not driven to despair; persecuted, but not abandoned; struck down, but not destroyed; always carrying about in the body the dying of Jesus, so that the life of Jesus may also be manifested in our body. For we who live are constantly being given up to death for the sake of Jesus, so that the life of Jesus may be manifested in our mortal flesh."
(2 Cor 4:7–11)

We were married on a sunny Saturday in July. You could call us college sweethearts, although we had only started dating at the end of senior year. But we were crazy in love. Our wedding day was everything we hoped: a beautiful Mass with family and friends, a delicious dinner at the reception, and a dance-floor-packed party late into the night. We left for our honeymoon in California the next morning, all our hope sweeping up into the sky on a shining jetliner. Life couldn't be sweeter.

Once we touched back down to normal life, reality became a bit bumpier. There were the natural growing pains of learning to live together and the ordinary stumbles of navigating jobs, graduate school, in-laws — even a new puppy. But we loved newlywed life: settling into our home together, enjoying date nights downtown, and celebrating the milestones of our first year.

From the beginning of our dating days, we had talked about wanting children. We came from similar families — four kids in Franco's, five in Laura's — and we thought something that size sounded good. At first we thought we would wait a few years before starting a family of our own. But early in our first year of marriage, our minds started to change. We found ourselves wondering whether God might be asking us to be open to a child sooner rather than later. After lots of prayer and conversation, we decided to try for a baby before we even pulled the wedding cake from the freezer to celebrate our first anniversary.

Pregnancy didn't happen as soon as we hoped. So Laura kept going to graduate school, figuring she could cut back to part-time whenever a baby arrived. But a baby didn't arrive. We passed the one-year mark of trying, waiting, and hoping. Officially we had entered into infertility. With the help of our natural family planning instructor, we were able to identify that Laura's irregular cycles were keeping us from conceiving. We saw doctors and specialists, tried vitamin supplements and special diets, and endured the ups and downs of fertility medications in the hopes of regulating Laura's cycles.

Nothing worked. Meanwhile friends, relatives, and coworkers were having babies left and right. Every week seemed to bring another pregnancy announcement. The news grew harder to take, our smiles harder to fake. Advent became especially heavy to bear, when the whole Church seemed to be happily waiting for a baby — while month after month, each pregnancy test turned up negative for us.

Infertility was a rough start to marriage. We wondered whether we would ever be able to conceive. We started researching adoption, but in our darker moments we doubted and even despaired. What if we never got to have a child at all? We tried to pray that God's will would be done, but in private each of us wrestled (and even raged) against the unfair hand we felt we had been dealt. Why would God place the desire for children in our hearts and then withhold them from us?

Then one dark December morning, two faint pink lines appeared in the test window. We could barely believe it: pregnant.

After nine months of holding our breath, we held our son Samuel. Every week of his infancy felt like a milestone, a miracle after a long wait. As we started settling into parenthood, we dared to let ourselves dream that maybe we would be able to have the family we hoped for.

When we decided to start trying for another baby, we were surprised to find it was much easier than the first time around. We were overwhelmed with gratitude to welcome our son Thomas, and we hoped our hard days were behind us. From the outside, everything looked ideal: two healthy kids, two years apart. People assumed we'd planned everything perfectly. But we knew it was far from our design — and our two gifts from God were nothing to take for granted.

Still, we started to let ourselves relax into a life that we assumed would continue on the same path: ordinary, everyday parenting. Which is why we were completely blindsided by miscarriage.

We never thought it would happen to us. Naively, we thought we had front-loaded our share of suffering on the infertility side of parenthood. But losing a longed-for baby changed everything we thought we knew. No longer was the positive pregnancy test the proof that we would hold a healthy baby in our arms nine months later. Everything felt tentative, shaky, and uncertain.

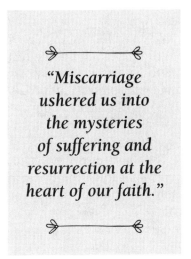

"Miscarriage ushered us into the mysteries of suffering and resurrection at the heart of our faith."

In the weeks and months following our miscarriage, the Scripture passage about "earthen vessels" (2 Cor 4:7–11) offered the verses we returned to again and again. We realized that a child's life was an infinite treasure, but one that could only be held in the vessel of bodies — bodies that are fragile and imperfect, bodies that can hold both life and death. Miscarriage ushered us into the mysteries of suffering and resurrection at the heart of our faith. Yet despite our grief and pain, our desire for another child only deepened through loss. We knew that God was calling us beyond fear to open our hearts again.

We decided to try for another baby as soon as our doctor said it was safe. Surprisingly, we were able to conceive on the next cycle, only six weeks after losing our baby. Pregnancy after miscarriage was a journey of faith, testing our trust as we tried to move past anxiety that we would lose this baby, too. Any time the slightest worry erupted, we had to choose to place our hope in God again. After what seemed like an endless wait, our son Joseph was born safely at full-term, and he felt like the miracle he was.

Life seemed wonderful again, redeemed in a powerful way. Our new baby was like the calm after a storm, and he brought such joy to our family. Despite the late nights and hard work of having a newborn in the house again, we saw in clearer light what a tremendous gift it was to welcome a child, even as we continued to remember and grieve the baby we had lost. We could never have imagined how God was preparing us to encounter even deeper mysteries of life and death with what came next, several years later.

When we learned Laura was pregnant again, we thought we knew what to expect. But at the first routine ultrasound, there were two heartbeats. Twins. Our lives flipped upside down as we tried to prepare for the prospect of two babies at once. Even though we felt overwhelmed, the legacy of infertility and miscarriage continued to bear fruit in our lives, reminding us that no challenge faced by having children could be greater than the prospect of losing them.

But the high-risk pregnancy became even more complicated. Once we learned the twins were identical and shared a placenta, Laura had to be monitored for twin-to-twin-transfusion syndrome, a rare complication in which one twin receives too much blood and one does not get enough. Unfortunately, the babies developed this life-threatening condition halfway through the pregnancy. After weeks of consulting with specialists, we decided to try in-utero surgery to severe the connected blood vessels in the placenta. But the surgery was unsuccessful, and the twins had to be delivered via C-section at twenty-four weeks gestation. Both babies went straight to the NICU where Franco baptized them, but they were too sick to survive.

Maggie lived one day. Abby lived two. Each girl died in our arms.

Their lives and deaths transformed us. Even as our family, friends, parish, and perfect strangers gathered around us in an incredible outpouring of the Body of Christ, our lives were turned inside out by grief. The trauma of birthing and burying two babies was almost too much to bear. We had to lean hard into our faith and each other to make it through each overwhelming day.

In the raw weeks of early grief, Franco had a powerful insight that brought us a sliver of hope. Since Maggie and Abby were created out of our love, our grief for them could never be greater than our love. (As an engineer he even had an equation for this proof: Love > Grief.) Even in the aftermath of their deaths, when we had been shaken to our core, we tried to trust that the God of love would not abandon us in our grief.

We never thought having babies would be this hard. But being open to life means being open to grief. We didn't understand this truth when we said "I do," but we learned it again and again in the years that followed. Vulnerability is part of love. We cannot choose to love without the possibility that our hearts might break along the way. But the risk of vulnerability is also what allows new life to be born.

Our marriage has experienced three deep griefs: infertility, miscarriage, and infant loss. Though we are far from the first or the last to suffer such sorrow, each encounter with loss has changed us in ways we never expected — as individuals and as a couple. We could never have dreamed that God could give us the strength or desire to open our hearts one more time to a child, even after so much loss. But a year and a half after Maggie and Abby's deaths, we returned to the same hospital to welcome our son Benjamin. Pregnancy after infant loss was even harder than after miscarriage, but with prayer and grace we made it through.

Not a day goes by when we do not think of each child we have been given, those under our roof and those home with God. Strangers smile and say, "Four boys?" Only we know the full story: that there are three more children in our family, forever in our hearts.

REFLECTION

If you haven't yet told the story of your pregnancy and miscarriage, use the space below to write down any memories, thoughts, or questions about your experience.

_____

_____

_____

_____

_____

_____

_____

_____

_____

_____

_____

_____

_____

_____

_____

_____

_____

_____

_____

Our Miscarriage

Laura's story

Our second son was turning two, and we loved imagining another child in our family. When we tried to conceive and it happened quickly, we were overjoyed. We had never forgotten our infertility days, so we did not take the gift for granted. We jumped right in, preparing for morning sickness and planning to surprise our families with the delightful news. After a few weeks of rejoicing privately, we decided to tell our kids and celebrate over ice cream. I took one more pregnancy test, just for kicks. Now there was only a hint of a line, barely there. Franco and I both frowned when we looked it. We knew it wasn't supposed to look like that.

I called my doctor to see if I could come in earlier for my first pre-natal appointment. When I went into the clinic the next day, the lab work showed my HCG levels were lower than they should have been for this point in pregnancy. The doctor thought maybe my dates were off, but we knew our date of conception. She thought things could still be fine, so she advised me to go home and see what happened.

The next day I was terrified. I told myself to keep hoping. But suddenly there was blood — a little, then a lot. I started crying and called Franco to ask him to come home from work. Then I called my mom and told her I was having a miscarriage, which was heart-breaking because I hadn't even gotten to tell her I was pregnant yet.

I didn't know what miscarriage would feel like or how fast it would progress. I figured that since I was still early in the pregnancy, miscarriage wouldn't be too painful. So I was overwhelmed when the cramping turned into contractions that felt like the worst of labor, slamming so fast I could barely breathe. I started shaking, and my arms and limbs went numb. I crawled to the phone and called the clinic. The nurse told me to get to the ER as fast as we could. Franco had to carry me downstairs to the car since I couldn't walk. I howled in pain the whole drive to the hospital, the same one where I had birthed my babies.

My memories of the emergency room are a blur of doctors and nurses trying to help as I lay there cramping, sweating, and shaking. Finally, the pain started to recede. A final ultrasound confirmed the baby was gone. Hours later we left with nothing but a bag of sanitary pads — a stark contrast to leaving the same hospital years before with a newborn tucked safely in the car seat.

The next morning, Franco's mom showed up at our front door with food. "I know how awful it is," she said, remembering her own miscarriage. "You feel like you're never going to get to meet your third child." In the weeks and months that followed, as I worked through my grief and wrote about losing our baby, this support and solidarity from others helped to carry me through. Even though my heart was broken, I knew I wasn't alone.

I soon realized that I needed to talk about our baby and the miscarriage more than Franco did. It didn't mean that he didn't love me or our child, just that he didn't process his grief the same way I did. I found a few blogs and online support groups for mothers who had lost babies, and it helped me so much to connect with other women who understood what I was feeling.

My mom also told me that praying to Mary had helped my grandma through her three miscarriages. That helped me a lot — to ask Mary to pray for me and to remember that Mary suffered so much in her motherhood out of love. It also helped me to connect with my grandma, to remember that she had lived through this same pain and yet was able to go on to have more children and hold fast to her faith.

In the early days and weeks after miscarriage, I wept all the time. I thought I would always have this dark cloud hanging over my life. I couldn't imagine ever feeling happy or hopeful again. Gradually, as time went on, my feelings became less intense — or maybe more familiar. I learned ways to cope, like taking a few moments to close my eyes and pray to God for the strength to get through what I was feeling. On the hard days when I knew I needed a good cry, I would listen to songs that reminded me of our baby. I could let out what I was feeling and then keep going. Now the hard days come around less frequently. I am grateful for that, even though I will always miss our baby.

Franco's story

When we first feared that Laura might miscarry, we had a glimmer of hope that it might just be an odd test result. We held onto that hope, praying that miscarriage wouldn't happen. I felt like this was so much of what our faith entails: believing in the impossible and trusting that God is greater than anything we could imagine, a wellspring of love and mercy, who will care for us always.

But when Laura called me at work and told me through sobs on the phone that she was miscarrying, I felt more hopeless and helpless than ever. It was a "walk out of the office and get home" moment. I knew that I had to get her to the hospital, but even that would not be enough to stop what was happening.

When we got to the ER, I was told I had to wait in the lobby until Laura had spent time in triage. This way the hospital staff could be sure that I hadn't precipitated the miscarriage and that she was "safe" with me around. I was angered that the staff would think I would do anything to my wife, but then I realized that hospitals don't ask that question without good cause.

Soon I was allowed to go to triage and be with her. She was starting to feel better physically by then, as most of the pain and cramping was past. While one of the nurses was in our room, a lullaby started playing over the PA system. She cheerily informed us that it meant that upstairs in labor and delivery, a baby had just been born. It was such terrible irony.

In the days and weeks after the miscarriage, the number of people who stopped by to ask about Laura was amazing. But I quickly realized that I could count on one hand the people that asked how I was doing. Responding with "We're grieving" or "We're doing ok" were often met with "But she was the one who was pregnant." This was one of the hardest things for me to experience. People never asked me about our miscarriage — they didn't even think to ask.

Finally, a few weeks after the miscarriage, a coworker came by and asked about it. We had an honest and sincere exchange, and he commented, "Wow, this almost makes we want to cry." I told him I did every day. Did my honesty about grieving make some people uncomfortable at times? Without question, it did. Do I regret it for a minute? Without question, I do not.

It has taken a long time for me to accept the feeling of powerless-ness that the miscarriage gave me. Losing the sense of control was something I had to grieve — even though I was never in control of whether our baby would live or not. My inability to stop the mis-carriage also turned into a heightened worry about my wife. In my vision as a husband who supports the family, I often found myself more concerned with how she was grieving than whether or not I was giving myself space to grieve. I felt like it was more important for me to be strong for her than to show her that I was grieving, too. This seemed like the right thing to do at the time, but actually made it harder for both of us. While I wasn't letting myself grieve in a healthy way, I was also presenting a larger contrast between the way Laura and I were grieving. This left her unsure if she was grieving more than I was, which wasn't the case.

Grief consumed me in unexpected ways. It was harder for me to cry than Laura. But I would find myself unable to have a coherent thought at work; I was just stuck in grief. I've also found myself at the bottom of a too-large bag of chips at hours of the night when nobody should be awake. I remember when a coworker — one of the nicest people I have ever met — told me his wife was pregnant. I was so jealous that I wanted to hit him in the face, a feeling I had never felt before. When grieving I've often wanted to destroy something (and breaking down cardboard boxes for recycling doesn't lessen the urge). As one friend related, "If I start cursing a blue streak in the morning because I spilled a cup of coffee, it's probably not about the coffee." But any time I have channeled my anger or grief into anything destructive, it leaves me exhausted, not feeling any better. Being constructive is better.

For me, grief often came in the quiet times when I was alone, frequently when I was in the car going to work. This uninterrupted quiet time was what worked best for me to reflect on the miscarriage and what it meant to me and my relationships with Laura and God. Being able to grieve alone allowed me to deepen my understanding of where I was in my grief — and gave me the time to form my thoughts and better articulate my emotions to Laura. I knew that our child being in the loving embrace of God instead of ours should not be a wedge driven between us.

CHAPTER 4

Your Grief as a Mother

"You formed my inmost being;
you knit me in my mother's womb.
I praise you, because I am wonderfully made;
wonderful are your works!
My very self you know.
My bones are not hidden from you,
When I was being made in secret,
fashioned in the depths of the earth.
Your eyes saw me unformed;
in your book all are written down;
my days were shaped, before one came to be."
(Ps 139:13–16)

Rare is the pregnant woman who doesn't worry about miscarriage. But we are the ones whose fears came true: the one in four women who have experienced pregnancy loss. Maybe you are a worrier who always frets that something will go wrong, so miscarriage was always a sinking fear in the back of your mind. Maybe you are an optimist, generally happy and hopeful, so the reality of this loss blindsided you. No matter your nature or temperament, the loss of your baby has likely affected you deeply — as a mother, a woman, a wife, and a person of faith.

We believe that God knit our babies together within us like a skilled weaver. God wrote the story of our child's life like a wise author. God shaped their days like clay in a potter's hands and created them in the dark like a seed in the depths of the earth. Because we love our children deeply as mothers, we grieve their death deeply, too. This chapter will look at our grief as women: grief's physical and emotional experiences, its impact on our identity and marriage, and stories of women in Scripture who can give us hope.

Physical experiences

While both parents have lost their child, mothers know the physical pain of loss most acutely. Chapter 1 describes the physical process and effects of miscarriage, but the emotional side of these experiences is equally important. Depending how recently your miscarriage happened, you may still be bleeding. Every time you use the bathroom, you are greeted with an unwelcome reminder of your loss. If your cycles have not yet returned, you may feel angry or betrayed by your body if you are hoping to try to conceive again. If you had a late term miscarriage or stillbirth, your milk may not yet have dried up, a painful reminder that your body longs for your baby as much as your heart.

As your breasts go back to their previous size and pregnancy symptoms like morning sickness disappear, you may feel sadness or relief. You may have trouble sleeping, have little appetite, and cry often. Or maybe you don't cry at all. There is no single or "right" way for women to grapple with their bodies and emotions in the wake of miscarriage.

You may still be wearing maternity clothes or bigger sizes to cover your stomach "showing." What was a happy baby bump a few days or weeks ago is now another inescapable reminder of your loss every time you change clothes, take a shower, or glance in the mirror.

When you still can't fit back in your regular pants, it feels like a cruel trick of nature — especially when you dread having a friend or stranger ask if you're pregnant.

Some women wish their body would go back to normal right away or see their stretch marks as painful reminders of what was. Others mourn when their pregnant belly disappears so quickly that it seems the baby never existed. Mothers often describe feeling a physical emptiness or ache for the child who is no longer there. You may hear baby cries that wake you at night, feel "phantom kicks," or have aching arms to hold the baby you have lost.

It can help to remember you are not alone in your suffering. Millions of women have struggled, often silently, through these same experiences. Leaving the hospital with no baby in the car seat. Sitting in a waiting room surrounded by pregnant bellies. Wondering how to answer questions like "how many children do you have?" Explaining to insurance providers that your baby died. Dreading small talk with the dental hygienist who asks about your pregnancy. Fearing a pregnancy announcement at family gatherings. Enduring a postpartum checkup with no baby in your arms. Struggling through Mass when babies are everywhere. Hearing others make insensitive jokes about pregnancy, children, or family size.

If you can find other women who have experienced a loss like yours, their stories can bring some comfort that you are never alone. The sisterhood of women who know this physical suffering and its emotional aftermath can offer you a lifeline to hold on to in the hardest moments. Ever since Eve, women have known the pain brought by bearing and birthing children. We cannot fix each other or take away this sorrow, but we can help carry each other through.

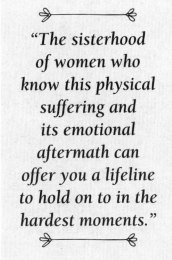

"The sisterhood of women who know this physical suffering and its emotional aftermath can offer you a lifeline to hold on to in the hardest moments."

Emotional experiences

Our emotions can consume our thoughts and hearts. Miscarriage is a complex experience, and you may feel everything from numbness to rage as you grieve. You might feel confused or conflicted, caught between extremes depending on the moment or your mood. Common emotional responses to miscarriage include:

- Anger: Why did this happen to me? Does God even care about me or my baby?
- Shock: How could this have happened? Is this real?
- Failure: Why couldn't my body care for my baby? Could I have done something to prevent this?
- Guilt: Was this my fault? Did we make the right medical decisions?
- Isolation: Does anyone understand how I'm feeling? Am I really a mother?
- Emptiness: How does my life still have meaning? Why doesn't anyone see how hard this is for me?
- Jealousy: Why do other women get to have babies so easily — even the ones who don't want them?
- Sadness: Will I ever feel happy again? Will grief always feel this heavy?

Mental health professionals offer the advice to "feel your feelings": to acknowledge and express your emotions without shame or judgment, rather than suppressing or feeling guilty about them. It can be helpful to have your feelings validated. The loss of a child is one of the hardest experiences that life can bring. But it can also be healing to know that your emotions do not define you. How you feel today is not necessarily how you will feel for the rest of your life. Especially when we are able to look upon our lives with eyes of faith, we remember the broader perspective that God is more powerful and enduring than any emotion.

It is important to pay attention to your mental health, since grief can become depression or anxiety that may require treatment from a professional. Postpartum depression, anxiety, and post-traumatic stress disorder can occur among women who have experienced miscarriage. (Anxiety can be even more common after miscarriage than depression.) You may wish to ask your husband or a trusted friend to help you monitor your mood and behavior by checking in with you regularly. If you experience a continued lack of interest in everyday life, loss of appetite, difficulty sleeping, inability to focus at work or home, withdrawal from friends and family, or intense sadness that makes it difficult to function, please contact your doctor and ask to be referred to a mental health professional for assistance. You can advocate for yourself, and you do not need to suffer alone. Seeking help is a sign of strength, not weakness. You are caring for yourself with the same attention and love you would give to your child.

Dealing with your grief

Managing your emotions can take many forms. Finding a trusted companion in whom you can confide is an important first step. Your husband, a friend, a family member, your pastor, a spiritual director, or a counselor can offer a listening ear and shoulder to cry on. While you should not feel pressured to share your feelings with anyone if you are not comfortable, it can bring relief to voice what is hurting within you. Having someone listen to you — especially in the early days when you may need to tell the story of your miscarriage over and over — can help to sort through how you are feeling. If you do not have someone in your life who can fill this role in person, you may wish to seek out an online support group for women grieving after miscarriage.

Another helpful approach to dealing with your emotions is to pay attention to what triggers your grief. Are there certain memories, smells, songs, people, places, or activities that seem to increase the intensity of your grieving? What can you do to avoid these triggers — or at least minimize your exposure to them?

Sometimes working to desensitize your grief response can help over time. For example, visiting the hospital or doctor's office can get easier if you start with shorter "exposures" under calmer circumstances. Other triggers may always provoke a flood of memories, so you may need to plan in advance how to cope. For example, excusing yourself to visit the restroom when friends or family make a surprise pregnancy announcement can be a way to let yourself react in private and then return to face others once you are ready. You might also ask a friend to stick close to your side and help field or deflect questions if you're not ready to talk about your miscarriage in public.

Other common grief triggers include social media, especially when it seems like everyone you know is expecting or has a baby. Instead of adding to your anxiety by worrying that you will see another ultrasound picture, consider ways to limit your time online or temporarily unfollow friends whose updates may be too painful for you right now. Making decisions to avoid grief triggers does not have to be permanent, but this approach can be helpful in the hardest weeks.

"*Mothering your own grieving heart is an act of love, too.*"

Baby showers can surface jealousy and longing as well. It is natural to feel envious or bitter when you have been robbed of your joy and innocence toward pregnancy. Give yourself the gift of being gentle with yourself, and consider if declining a shower invitation might be a better decision than putting yourself through the agony of attending. You can always send a gift in advance with your prayers and well wishes. Mothering your own grieving heart is an act of love, too.

As a mother

For many women, their identity starts to shift as soon as they learn they are expecting. While men may grow into their new identity as a father gradually, either later in the pregnancy (once they can feel the baby kick or learn the gender) or after the baby is born, women often feel like their motherhood began the day they saw a positive pregnancy test. Miscarriage can therefore bring immediate emotional trauma to the mother, while the father may take longer to acknowledge his grief or prefer to grieve privately. (Reading chapter 5 about fathers' grief may help you to understand this perspective.)

If you are single and miscarry your baby, you may feel guilt or judgment from others that clouds and complicates your grief. Too often single mothers have suffered in silence, or worse, in shame. But you are not alone: many women have stood in your shoes, struggling with mourning their baby and trying to heal while people around them pressure them to move on and forget about their past. You may even find that some people are relieved that the "problem" has been taken care of — words that dismiss your baby and shut down your ability to grieve. You may find it helpful to seek out online support groups where you can share freely about your baby and connect with other mothers who understand the particular challenges of your grief. Seeking out a compassionate priest, lay minister, or counselor can be another important source of support and comfort.

If you do not have other living children, you may feel conflicted about your identity when people do not identify you as a mother since your child is not visible here with you. Some women describe feeling like an "almost-mother" after miscarriage. The truth that our faith upholds is that your baby was a real person with a unique soul, created and loved by God from the moment of his or her conception. Even if the world does not acknowledge this fact, the deeper realities held by faith will endure longer than any earthly perspective. You are indeed the mother of this child and will be forever.

As a wife

Women sometimes feel frustrated with their husband's response to the loss of their baby. "Why isn't my husband sadder?" you may wonder. "Why doesn't he want to talk about our baby?" You might be an "attender" to your grief: someone who actively attends to their emotions in grief, finding comfort and healing by immersing themselves in the reality of their loss. Your husband, on the other hand, may be a "distractor": someone who deals with loss by turning to other projects to keep from feeling overwhelmed by the enormity of grief. Regardless of which spouse may be inclined toward being an attender or a distractor, it is hard when you are on drastically different pages in grief. You can start to feel isolated if you fear that your spouse doesn't understand you or doesn't care as deeply about the miscarriage as you do. (Ideas for connecting with your husband are found in chapter 6.)

Society holds sharply different expectations for women and men around grief. Crying is considered acceptable for women, but not for men. Expressing emotions is seen as feminine, while staying strong and stoic is considered more masculine. You may find that such tendencies run true for you and your husband, or you may find them to be stereotypes that don't fit your relationship. Either way, you will likely encounter such cultural expectations — whether people feel you are grieving "too much" or not enough. Remember that God created your heart to love, and we grieve because we love. How you choose to express your grief is a deeply personal decision, and no one has the right to tell you how to grieve.

Models of faith

As women, our bodies were created by God to carry life. Yet as mothers who have lost babies, we know the shadow side of motherhood, too. The death of a child can bring a crisis of faith. As you pray through your grief, you may find it helpful to turn to stories of women from Scripture who suffered because of fertility issues. Reflecting on a Scripture verse that speaks to your heart can remind you how God is reaching out to you in your pain, even if you don't find the exact answers to your difficult questions.

Scripture gives us stories of many women who grieved in their journey to have children. Rachel struggled with envy — for her sister Leah, who was able to conceive easily (Gn 30:1–24). The complicated relationships between Rachel, Leah, and Jacob speak to the intense emotions of desiring a child: anger, frustration, competition, and desperation. Hannah poured out her grief in lament to God when she was infertile (1 Sm 1:1–2:11). The depth of her sorrow and the strength of her faith were revealed in her lament at her infertility and later in her song of joy when she praised God for the gift of her son, Samuel.

Stories from both the Old and New Testaments also reveal God's power to work beyond ordinary expectations and the normal limits of fertility. Even after God's promise to her husband Abraham, Sarah could not believe she would ever have a child after decades of trying and jealousy at her maidservant Hagar, who bore Abraham a son (Gn 18:9–14). When she finally conceived and gave birth to a son in her old age, she described how Isaac's name (related to the word for laughter) captured both her joy and her disbelief (Gn 21:1–8). Elizabeth thought herself barren and too old for a child, yet the angel Gabriel surprised her husband, Zechariah, with news of a son. The strange circumstances surrounding the birth of John the Baptist brought both rejoicing and fear among their neighbors and relatives (Lk 1:5–25, 57–80). Reading stories of these sisters of faith can offer solidarity and empathy — that women have long wrestled with God over their desire to bear children and that God heard their cries with compassion.

Above all, Mary the Mother of God knows what it means to lose a child. Suffering was the sword that pierced her heart (Lk 2:35). Mary's path to motherhood looked nothing like she could have imagined. From the moment the angel Gabriel announced startling news, she learned that all her plans would be turned upside down. Saying yes to God ultimately meant watching Jesus suffer and die. The image of Mary holding the body of her son in Michelangelo's *Pietà* captures the anguish of a mother's broken heart. Mary had to trust — despite all evidence to the contrary — that God would bring new life from death.

The psalms speak to the emotions of grief in a powerful way:

> I am wearied with sighing;
>> all night long I drench my bed with tears;
>> I soak my couch with weeping....
>> The Lord has heard the sound of my weeping.
> The Lord has heard my plea;
>> the Lord will receive my prayer. (Psalm 6:7, 9b–10)

The power of lament in Scripture is that this form of prayer not only speaks to the fullness of human suffering, but always returns to faith in God — the hope and trust that co-exist with sorrow and pain. The psalms remind those who mourn that we can bring all of our emotions and questions to God. Nothing needs to be hidden from the Lord who made us and created our beloved children out of love.

REFLECTION QUESTIONS

How has the loss of your baby affected you as a woman? As a wife? As a mother?

What is one thing you wish you could tell your husband about your grief?

Caroline and Matt's story

On Mother's Day, I was nineteen weeks pregnant with our fifth child when I realized that I hadn't felt the baby move in a while. I hid my growing fear while celebrating with my husband and children. The next day I stopped into the doctor's office to put my fears at ease, but instead they confirmed through ultrasound that our baby was gone. I had to call my husband and tell him: "There is no heartbeat." Telling our children was devastating.

The next morning, I went to the hospital to be induced. I didn't want to let my baby go. Labor was just like my other births, so I was in a lot of pain. The anesthesiologist came for my epidural and told me that I was "lucky" and "should just be grateful" to have kids at home. Thanks be to God, that moment was tempered by our wonderful Catholic nurse who was so kind and understanding. I delivered our beautiful tiny son, Maximilian Francis, that afternoon. Upon seeing him, a peace washed over me. No doubt this was a grace from God.

Our children wanted to meet this sweet baby that they had talked to and prayed for every day of his little life. We all spent several hours with him, wondering at his tininess and perfection. We took pictures and said hello and goodbye. We took hand and foot prints, and we all held him. Our priest came and did a blessing. This time was surreal and such a blur. One moment you are pregnant and anxiously anticipating the arrival of a new baby. The next moment you are planning a funeral.

Grief hit immediately, but moving forward was the hardest. Everyday life was so difficult. Getting out of bed and going about my daily routine took all my energy. So many things triggered my grief, like a certain song on the radio. I had to plan my shopping trips to avoid the baby aisle. At one of my follow-up appointments, I was in the waiting room with a woman who had a newborn, and I had to wait in the hallway.

Next to my own grief, seeing my children grieve the loss of their brother was the hardest thing I've ever done. The doctors could give no reason why Max had died. Some days it helped to know this. Other days it haunted me.

When I went to the hospital to deliver Max, I fell apart as the nurse took us to our room. "I don't want to be here" was all I could manage to get out. I have felt this so often since. Especially in early grief, the weight of this cross felt too heavy, oppressive, and never-ending. Someone told me once that you don't "get over" the loss of your baby, but you become stronger under the weight of this cross. I am finding this to be true as the years pass. I wish someone had told me this sooner — that I would get stronger, that I would never forget or stop loving him but that I would smile again, laugh again, and find joy. Those things felt so far away in the beginning.

In the weeks following our loss, so many people reached out with stories of their own miscarriages and stillbirths. I had no idea I knew so many who had suffered through this. Our family and friends were very supportive, even though many of them didn't know what to say. We were comforted by those who validated our grief.

But shortly after I delivered Max, we moved to another state and found ourselves far from our supportive friends and family. A friend had added me to a baby loss group online, but I needed the support of other Catholic women who had been through this. So I started the "Mommy To A Little Saint" Facebook group. I never could have guessed what the Holy Spirit would do with this group. God has brought such beauty and healing to so many women. Today thousands give and receive support and prayers through this group. Every life has a purpose no matter how short their lives were, and I have no doubt that this is part of my son's purpose. Helping others through their grief has helped me to deal with mine.

Every day I hear stories of women suffering through grief alone. At best some are ignored; others are downright shamed for grieving their babies. Baby loss is a taboo subject in our society. Our churches should be a place of understanding and support. When Catholic families are open to life, they often experience loss. What are we as a Church doing to help those dealing with miscarriage, stillbirth, and infant loss? After we lost Max, it was hard for me to participate in pro-life activities because I was angry. There was such sadness surrounding babies lost to abortion and special places honoring those losses in our churches. But where were the tears and memorials for all the babies who were loved, wanted, and lost? I pray that those of us who feel strong enough to be vocal about our losses will help spur on this change in our own parishes.

Not long after we lost our son, my husband felt called to try for another child. I was terrified — of losing another baby and of having our living children grieve again. If it had been up to me alone, I don't think I would have ever been ready. But I trusted my husband. In the week of my original due date with Max, we found out we were pregnant. It was scary, and emotionally I was a wreck. Our twenty-week ultrasound wasn't as reassuring as we had hoped, and the fear continued. Our baby was small like Max had been, and she wasn't moving as often as she should. My constant prayer was "God, please just let her live. We will take her any way she comes!"

We prayed the novena to Our Lady Undoer of Knots, begging her intercession. Our daughter was born a month early on the anniversary of her brother's funeral Mass, which we took as a sign that her big brother was looking out for her. She was born with the longest cord our doctor had ever seen and had two "true knots" in her cord. We believe Our Lady literally undid the effect of those knots.

CHAPTER 5

Your Grief as a Father

"The LORD, your God, who goes before you, is the one who will fight for you, just as he acted with you before your very eyes in Egypt, as well as in the wilderness, where you saw how the LORD, your God, carried you, as one carries his own child, all along your journey until you arrived at this place." (Dt 1:30–31)

As husbands we often picture ourselves as the ones that go before our families: to take care of our wife, to keep our children safe, and to be there when they need us. We may take pride in making sure that we are the last one out the door when leaving the house, the last to fill our dinner plate, or the one to check the doors and turn off the lights before bed. Husbands and fathers often see their role in this way: to be the rock of the family, to make sure that everybody else is cared for and that things go as planned. Men can be stereotyped as the strong, silent type: always there but never in the spotlight.

Miscarriage puts us in that same role — present but not in the spotlight — only with an often overwhelming sense of helplessness. No matter how much careful preparation and planning was done, this pregnancy did not go as planned. In addition to the loss of your baby and the secondary loss of the hopes and dreams of who your baby would become, there is also the loss of knowing that much of life is out of your control.

The death of your child is not what you wanted to happen to your life, your marriage, or your wife. If you take pride in being steady and calm whenever anyone needs help, it can be hard when suddenly you feel lost or need your own rock while trying to support your family in their grief.

Physical and emotional experiences

Men experience many of the same emotions as women after miscarriage: sadness, anger, frustration, numbness, depression, or jealousy. Right now you may be concerned with trying to take care of your wife in her pain. You might feel helpless for not being able to keep your baby safe. You may feel listless or ambivalent at work, unable to focus. You might not want to get out of bed, or you might feel like shouting at anyone who crosses your path.

The word "grief" comes from the Latin *gravis*, meaning heavy, hard, serious, or sad. True to its roots, grief can be heavy and surprisingly exhausting. But husbands also carry the added concern about their wife's physical and emotional health — and they lack the support that mothers typically receive after the loss of a baby.

People often, and almost exclusively, express concern for the mother after a miscarriage. A father's grief can feel forgotten and marginalized. Research shows that a father's grief after the loss of a baby is often minimized or dismissed. Health care providers ask about the mother's physical and emotional health, but rarely ask about the father. Yet studies show that men have heightened rates of anxiety after the loss of a baby and can be at risk for post-traumatic stress just like women. Many fathers say that they wish they had better support after losing their child.

While fathers do not share in the physical experiences of pregnancy or miscarriage, they can still have strong visceral reactions to loss. Grief for men can be manifested physically as stress, exhaustion, insomnia, weight gain, or loss of appetite. They may try to escape from grief by diving back into work, exercising, indulging in TV or video games, or self-medicating through alcohol, drugs, or other addictions. Men sometimes bury their grief, hoping it will disappear if they ignore it — but unresolved grief usually resurfaces later down the road.

Dealing with your grief

Our society sends messages to men about expressing their feelings from the time they are young boys: "Real men don't cry." "Don't be a sissy." "Man up." As a result of what men are taught — explicitly or unconsciously — about grief, fathers may appear more stoic or less emotional after loss. You may find that you want to return to work and get back into normal routines sooner than your wife. You may not want to talk about your feelings as much as she does. Don't feel guilty if your grief feels smaller than your wife's. You may simply need more time to process, or your grief may manifest itself in different ways.

One of the most important things you can do is give yourself the space to let all of your emotions into your life. You may not want to deal with them at any given time, but you will almost always feel worse if you try to ignore a grief-filled moment, hoping to avoid it. Experts say you heal more fully if you let yourself enter completely into the emotions of grief. For example, you may feel uncomfortable hearing a line from a reading or hymn at Mass that puts a lump in your throat and a tear in your eye. But if you let yourself accept this emotion as a reminder of your love for your child, you can acknowledge the reality of this loss and pray to God for the strength and hope to keep going.

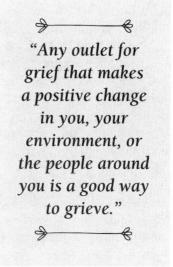

"Any outlet for grief that makes a positive change in you, your environment, or the people around you is a good way to grieve."

While you cannot fix what happened, you can still help your wife in many ways after miscarriage: communicate with family and friends about what has happened, contact your pastor, make burial arrangements, or deal with medical bills. Doing something active also helps your spouse to see that you are grieving, too. There is comfort in knowing that you are doing your best to grieve in the way that seems most natural. It is not always easy, especially if you have not experienced grief like this before. But if you are honest with God about your feelings as you care for yourself and others, you can trust that the Lord will help you to grieve well.

You have the right to honor your baby in the best way you can. Some men pick up a notebook and write or spend time in prayer or adoration, while others take up the task of handling the logistics surrounding their loss. Any outlet for grief that makes a positive change in you, your environment, or the people around you is a good way to grieve.

In grieving, many men find themselves wanting to do something constructive. You might want to plant a tree in your baby's honor, make a memorial garden, build a box for keepsakes, or start a fund-raising effort in honor of your child. These are all ways you can create a new memory and feel proud as a father.

As a father

You have as much right to grieve as your wife, because you are the father of this child. Your loss is great, and it deserves to be treated this way. Allowing yourself to grieve helps you to work through the loss and take care of yourself in a healthy way. This will ultimately help you to be the husband and father you want to be.

Nobody questions a new father for showing picture after picture of a newborn. The outward expression of his love is obvious and acceptable. You, too, were imagining and dreaming of a future as a father of this baby. You did not get the chance to get a nursery ready, to build the crib and paint the room, but you can still channel that feeling into doing something positive for your wife or in honor of your child. Grieving your loss, in whatever way works best for you, is truly the same thing: an outward expression of your love for the baby you lost.

As a husband

You may wonder why your wife is grieving so hard or for so long. Reading chapter 4 about mothers' grief may help you to understand more about your wife's perspective. People often say that "men and women grieve differently," but the truth is that every individual grieves differently. Noticing and communicating how you and your wife are coping is helpful because it gives the freedom to grieve in your own way, at your own time. Your hearts have been broken by the same tragedy but will heal differently and at different speeds. You can meet in the truth that for both of you, there will be days when the scar will be stretched and grief will rise up again.

Your wife likely needs to hear that you feel sad or miss the baby, too. Sharing some of your emotions with her can be a huge help for her own grief. But if talking about the miscarriage with her feels too hard, you could try opening up to another dad or a friend who has also experienced grief in his life (even if it is not the loss of a baby). Statistically speaking, so many couples have experienced miscarriage that it is likely you have a friend, coworker, or family member who has gone through this, too.

Over time you may find small ways to remember your baby with your wife. This may be as simple as sending her a card or flowers on the anniversary of the miscarriage or praying together in a special way on that day. For some men, talking about the miscarriage remains difficult but sending an email or text message to say that you love your wife and are thinking of your baby can let her know how much you love them both.

Models of faith

In contrast to the negative messages about grief that men receive today, our faith has powerful stories of men who grieve. The entire Book of Job tells of a husband and father trying to understand his life and faith after the loss of everything he loves. King David also grieved the loss of a child — under very different circumstances but with the same intense grief that many of us feel after miscarriage: "David pleaded with God on behalf of the child. He kept a total fast, and spent the night lying on the ground clothed in sackcloth. The elders of his house stood beside him to get him to rise from the ground; but he would not, nor would he take food with them" (2 Sm 12: 16–17).

The story of Jesus weeping at the death of his friend Lazarus reminds us all that it is okay to grieve openly, and that God grieves with us: "When Mary came to where Jesus was and saw him, she fell at his feet and said to him, 'Lord, if you had been here, my brother would not have died.' When Jesus saw her weeping and the Jews who had come with her weeping, he became perturbed and deeply troubled, and said, 'Where have you laid him?' They said to him, 'Sir, come and see.' And Jesus wept" (Jn 11:32–35).

The psalms of lament do not hold back in speaking honestly about sorrow and anger to God:

> Be gracious to me, LORD, for I am in distress;
>> affliction is wearing down my eyes,
>> my throat and my insides....
> I am forgotten, out of mind like the dead;
>> I am like a worn-out tool....
> But I trust in you, LORD;
>> I say, "You are my God." (Ps 31:10, 13, 15)

For thousands of years the psalms have helped grieving Christians turn to God in the hardest situations. Christ himself cried out the words of Psalm 22 on the cross: "My God, my God, why have you forsaken me?" (Mt 27:46). Especially if you are struggling with doubt or anger toward God, the psalms can help you feel less alone.

Saints who understand a father's grief can also be a source of support. Saint Paulinus of Nola (a friend of Saint Augustine's) was married and after many years without children, he and his wife Therasia had a son who died a week after birth. This devastating loss led the couple to retreat from the world and give away their wealth in order to lead a more devout life. In his letters, Saint Paulinus wrote, "It is a loving act to show sadness when our dear ones are torn from us, but it is a holy act to be joyful through hope and trust in the promises of God.... Granted our love may weep for a time, but our faith must ever rejoice. We should long for those who have been sent before us, but we should not lose hope of gaining them back." (See chapter 9 for more saints who grieved the loss of their children.)

REFLECTION QUESTIONS

How has the loss of your baby affected you as a husband? As a father?

What is one thing you wish you could tell your wife about your grief?

Nancy's story

I was only taking the pregnancy test to humor my husband. He was on a work trip and was tired of my complaining of fatigue and nausea. "Sounds like you're pregnant," he said. "Not possible," I said. Yet there it was. Two bold red lines.

Outside the bathroom door, my children were squabbling, ready for baths and bed. We already had three babies, the oldest not yet four, the baby only nine months. I was tired, overwhelmed by screaming and diapers, and not in any way ready to be doing it all while pregnant once again. Besides, we had really tried — for the first time in our marriage — to not get pregnant for a cycle. Just one cycle. And we had failed.

I stared at those lines, and disbelief melted into anger. This could not be happening! I thought I knew how to chart! I can't do another pregnancy right now! Were we just never going to be able to have sex again? Was I ever going to get a break between pregnancies? Did I have no say in any of this?

I was mad. Mad at God, mad at the Church, mad at myself. Mad that this little one, already growing inside of me, was greeted like this. I wept for a week. Even as I lay there crying, I knew that I wasn't weeping about the difficulties of pregnancy or being overwhelmed with little ones. I wept because I felt completely powerless. I wept because I had no control.

It took me two weeks to accept this pregnancy, my fourth in less than five years of marriage. When I did accept it, I felt a great surrender in my soul, and along with that came a great joy. It arrived suddenly: a wonderful peace. This baby was not our plan, but instead this baby was God's plan. I felt certain I was part of something greater. So we rejoiced in this new life.

We announced the pregnancy to our friends and family, but that same afternoon I started to bleed. I went in for an ultrasound a few days later and saw a perfect little active nine-week baby. But by that evening the bleeding increased. It was clear I was no longer pregnant, that the baby was no longer there. We were devastated.

It is hard to pull neat lessons out of real-life experiences, and to be honest I'm still sorting all of this out. But I feel quite changed by all that happened. We named the baby Peter. He will forever be a part of our family and a part of our story.

Two months after the loss, we intentionally got pregnant. We welcomed that baby in May. Loss and lessons learned don't make this life easier. They do, however, make things more clear. Having held and lost a fragile little one in my womb opened my eyes to the wonder and miracle of everything we experience during these years of fertility. When we lose that sense of wonder, we begin to think we can control — that we have a right to control — the mystery. NFP offers us science that works in conjunction with our bodies and allows us to play a greater role in the formation of our families. But it leaves the door open to God, and it leaves the control, ultimately, with Him.

Bill's story

It was 2:00 a.m. The phone rang suddenly, waking me up. It was Nancy trying to FaceTime with me. I was away on a work trip. I answered and was greeted with my wife's sobbing face, nearly hysterical. I could barely make it out at first, but I slowly understood. She was pregnant. She kept repeating it. She was distraught because we were really trying to practice NFP. We had decided it was best for all of us to put a little space between our youngest child and the next baby. Sure, we knew we wanted more children, but having so many this young felt really daunting.

I listened to her cry, trying to fight back my own disappointment. We should be happy about this! How did we mess up? What went wrong? All those powerful suggestions that the devil whispers in your ear when things like this happen.

After we hung up, I sat at the end of the bed trying to grasp what she just told me and how this new baby would affect our lives. I was stuck on how tough it would be, wondering if we could really do it. Then, all of a sudden, I felt this really warm feeling, this great sense of peace. I knew then that it was the Lord showing me that we are subject to His plan and not our own. This little life was a reminder that being open to life really means being open.

I felt so humbled and happy. I immediately called Nancy back and told her what I was experiencing. I told her how much I loved her and that this was a good thing and not to be upset or frustrated, that the Lord saw fit to bless us in a way so many people struggle to be blessed.

I returned home that weekend, and later in the week Nancy lost the baby. I couldn't believe it. After all the emotion and comfort and excitement, how could this be happening? Our child was gone just as quickly as he came. I hate to admit it, but I never thought this would happen to us. I guess that was the lesson I was intended to learn: that we aren't impervious to these things, and life won't always go along like expected.

I'm not sure I ever expected to have four or more children until I fell in love with Nancy. Through the grace I have been so fortunate to receive from my wife and from my Lord, I am truly committed to life and living our marriage in a way that is open to life. If that commitment brings sorrow along with it, I am not scared because I know the Lord is showing us the path He intends for us. We just need to be open to following it.

CHAPTER 6

Grieving as a Couple

"Blessed are they who mourn, for they will
be comforted." (Mt 5:4)

Your child was with you in this world, although for too short a time. Your mourning is rooted in the truth that this blessing existed: that your child was here. Grief is one of the tangible reminders that your baby was a blessing in your lives. The promise of comfort is often hard to comprehend when grief is great. But you can take solace in knowing that the boundless compassion of God is always present to those who mourn.

The challenge — and the promise — of grieving as a couple is that you are going through this loss together. Together you are bereaved parents: "bereaved" meaning bereft, robbed, or deprived of something important or close. Together you share this loss, even though you experience it differently as husband and wife. This means that you may each question at times why your spouse isn't responding in the same way as you. This chapter seeks to help you understand the differences and similarities between your grief as spouses and ultimately strengthen your marriage through loss.

Differences in a couple's grieving

Grieving is emotionally and physically exhausting, especially in the early days or on difficult anniversaries. Exhaustion can magnify any communication challenges that already exist. In the beginning, the dynamic of your relationship may feel more like "parallel grief" alongside each other. You may collapse together at the end of the day but feel too drained to talk. You might enjoy small distractions like watching a favorite show or movie together. But you might also feel torn between your own needs and your spouse's, worrying about bringing them down when you need to talk.

"Navigating the uneven terrain of couple's grief can be tricky, even with the best intentions."

Couples can quickly feel out of sync after loss. One of you may want to talk about your baby regularly; the other never seems to bring up the subject. One spouse might want to research the causes of miscarriage; the other seems to accept what has happened. One of you might want to visit the cemetery; the other not at all. The extrovert wants to go out with friends to cheer up; the introvert needs to stay in and crawl into bed early. You may find that you fight more often or lose your temper more quickly. Navigating the uneven terrain of couple's grief can be tricky, even with the best intentions.

Men and women also experience different treatment after miscarriage. Starting with doctors and nurses, many people neglect the father's grief and focus instead on the mother. External pressures of how to grieve — from family, friends, coworkers, or society — can make you question if your grief is "right" or "wrong" according to what people expect from a man or woman.

Because grief is expressed individually, natural differences in the ways couples grieve can come from a variety of sources:

- Contrasts in personality or temperament
- Societal stereotypes or cultural differences in how men and women should grieve
- Expectations of family and friends
- Differences in religious practices, whether in belief (if you belong to different faiths) or habit (if you prefer different practices of prayer)

Each of these differences can pose challenges for your relationship in grief, for example:

- If one spouse is an introvert and the other is an extrovert
- If no one expects the husband to grieve, or if people feel the mother is grieving too much
- If relatives or friends pressure you to "get over it" or "get back to normal"
- If you do not share the same religion or if one of you faces a crisis of faith

Grief is as unique as the soul of the child that you lost. There is no right way to grieve. Some people mourn quietly, others more publicly. But you can make grief worse if you do not give yourself or your partner the opportunity to deal with this loss. Trying to push away or bury grief rarely works. If you do not find some outlet to express or communicate your pain, it can create bigger problems down the road. Unresolved or delayed grief often erupts later in life, becoming even harder to handle. You may find that it helps to take advantage of moments when grief feels less heavy to check in with your partner about how they are feeling. Letting them know that you care about their well-being is essential.

Women tend to be "intuitive grievers" who are more comfortable expressing emotions, while men are often "instrumental grievers" who prefer to act or problem-solve. We each need to mourn in the way that is right for us while honoring the grief of our partner. It takes patience and plenty of communication to figure out what is best for you as husband and wife. Remember that grief is normal. The loss and pain that happened may feel unnatural, but grieving is natural. We grieve because we love.

Ways to cope

Especially when your grief is raw and new, seeking out sources of comfort and community can start to help you see a way forward. Reaching out to family, friends, or a trusted pastor can free your spouse from feeling like they must provide all your emotional support. Many couples have also been helped through grief counseling. A trained therapist can help you to examine your relationship as husband and wife, your families of origin, past experiences of loss, different cultural expectations around grief, and common responses to the particular loss you have experienced. A pregnancy or infant loss support group can be another positive source of support, helping you understand how to be companions to each other even through your differences.

As parents, you each have your own unique relationship to the child that you lost. This list of ways to process your grief — some action-oriented, some feeling-oriented — can help you to support each other:

- Pray for or with your spouse
- Spend time alone
- Spend time with others
- Reflect on favorite prayers or Scripture verses
- Listen to music
- Write a letter to express your emotions — to your baby, to your spouse, or to God
- Exercise or take a walk
- Journal or write
- Spend time in nature
- Go to Mass or adoration
- Make a memorial garden, build a keepsake box, or start a

home improvement project
- Paint or draw
- Plan a weekend away to enjoy a change of scenery
- Read about other people's experiences of miscarriage or other losses
- Look at keepsakes that remind you of your baby (photos from the pregnancy, emails or texts about the pregnancy, or items from the hospital)

Paying attention to what helps your grief can show you how to move forward. Noticing what activities or relationships give you strength, peace, or comfort can point to what to keep doing. Likewise, identifying people, places, or activities that deplete your energy and leave you feeling worse can signal what to avoid.

Particular challenges

Miscarriage happens in every situation imaginable. Some parents lose their first baby, while others lose an unplanned pregnancy or experience multiple losses. For many the miscarriage comes soon after they find out they are pregnant; others learn their baby has died halfway through the pregnancy. Couples who lose a "honeymoon baby" must deal with the sudden shift from the joy of the wedding to the sorrow of loss. Couples who were trying to conceive for years are devastated by miscarriage after infertility. Situations like molar pregnancy and chemical pregnancy can leave couples feeling confused about how to mourn.

When the baby you lost was your first child
- You may face shock that your pregnancy could end in loss.
- You may feel like you are not "really" a parent according to society's definition.
- You may find comfort in the truth that our faith affirms the life of your child from the moment of conception — and thus affirms you as a parent as well.

When the miscarriage was early
- You may face the sadness of telling friends and family about

your miscarriage when you hadn't even announced the pregnancy yet.

- You may feel lost without physical evidence of your baby's existence, like an ultrasound photo.
- You may find comfort in remembering that you have the right to mourn your baby and that grief is not defined by how long you were pregnant.

When the pregnancy wasn't planned

- You may face guilt that you were not joyful or excited about your pregnancy.
- You may feel regret or fear that you are being punished.
- You may find comfort in knowing that your response to the miscarriage does not depend on your emotions during the pregnancy: you can still love and mourn this baby, no matter how you first reacted to the news that you were expecting.

When you have had multiple miscarriages

- You may face the physical toll that multiple losses can take on your body, as well as the emotional roller coaster of grief overload.
- You may feel increasing anger, jealousy, anxiety, or despair with each loss — or you may become numb and discouraged.
- You may find comfort in consulting a NaPro-trained physician about treatments for recurrent miscarriage that can be more effective than conventional infertility treatments.

When you have other living children

- You may face the added burden of explaining this loss to your living children and dealing with their questions, emotions, and grief on top of your own.
- You may feel guilt for grieving when you have healthy, living children, feeling that your focus should be on gratitude for what you have.
- You may find comfort in including the baby you lost whenever you pray for or with your children, to remember they

will always remain part of your family.

When your miscarriage involves the loss of one or more multiples

- You may face the complicated grief of mourning multiple children or continuing with a pregnancy when one of the babies has already died.
- You may feel pressure to focus on the living baby (or babies) if you have experienced vanishing twin syndrome. If you have lost all the babies in your pregnancy, you may mourn the prospect of having twins or triplets and the special identity of being a parent of multiples.
- You may find comfort in connecting with an online support group for the loss of multiples, to find other parents who understand this unique and complex grief.

How to support your children

If you have living children, you will need to decide how to explain the miscarriage to them. Using age-appropriate language is important for sharing the news at their level. For younger children, it may be enough to say that Mommy and Daddy were going to have another baby, but the baby died so now he or she is in heaven with God. Your family can pray to your little saint and ask them to pray for you, and they will always be part of your family. Mommy and Daddy are sad, but even tears are a sign of love. It is okay to talk about and miss your baby or to picture them in heaven with Jesus and Mary. Children may find comfort in drawing family pictures that show the baby, including the baby in your prayers at night, or lighting a candle for your baby at church.

For older children, you may have to explain further as they will likely have more questions — what was wrong with the baby, where the baby went, why God let this happen, or if they will get to see the baby when they get to heaven. You may wish to explain that the baby's body might not have been healthy or strong enough to live outside the womb. In terms of questions of faith, you can answer simply and honestly, knowing that you do not need to have all the answers. You can talk about how faith means believing and trusting in God even in the hardest times, even when we do not understand why bad things happen. You may wish to ask your pastor to speak with your children, too, or to offer your family a special blessing as a way to show them that God's love still surrounds them even in their grief.

Letting kids know that it is okay to be sad, angry, or confused is an important step to creating a healthy environment in your home around grief. Children often process their emotions through regressive behaviors or acting out, so it is common to see a negative impact on your child's behavior, especially in the first days and weeks after the miscarriage. If you are concerned about your child, contact their pediatrician or a trained child psychologist to help answer your questions.

How to support each other

Miscarriage evokes a wide range of emotions: sadness, depression, helplessness, numbness, or confusion. Anger can be an especially challenging emotion, as you may find the target of your anger shifting — to your spouse, family, friends, medical personnel, strangers, or God. It can be easy to be short-tempered with those closest to you. Yet isolation can be the most alienating and divisive emotion for a marriage. You can become self-absorbed and lack the energy to engage your spouse's needs. Or you may worry that your spouse is "over" their grief and does not care as much about the miscarriage as you do. Contrasts or conflicts in how we grieve can lead us to fear that we are alone.

At its best, grieving as a couple is done with empathy for what your partner is going through — especially when your emotions are different from theirs. Empathetic grieving means giving your spouse the space and time they need. It means being intentional about communicating with each other. It means allowing yourself to be vulnerable to the one you love and trusting that your honesty will be met with compassion.

Sitting down and talking every night is the solution for some couples, while quietly introspecting is the key for others. For the majority of couples, however, the best path lies somewhere in the middle. Finding the method and frequency of communication is part of the work of grieving in marriage. Just as you were partners in pregnancy, so you can become partners in grief.

Remember that any differences in how you grieve are still small compared to the heartache of losing your baby — so you can strive to find comfort in your shared love for each other and your child. The most important choice you can make is when and how to turn to God and to each other. It is a choice that couples have to make actively and regularly, even years after miscarriage.

If you and your spouse have different faith backgrounds or beliefs, you may encounter conflicts in your understandings of God's role in your child's death or what heaven will be like. Giving each other respect and space to communicate your beliefs can be challenging for such emotional subjects, but you can always return to the love you share for each other and for your child. Praying for the strength to love your spouse where they are — and for God's grace to continue growing in faith — can ultimately bear fruit for your marriage.

REFLECTION QUESTIONS

What part of your spouse's grief have you struggled to understand?

In what ways have you grieved similarly or differently?

What has been helpful for your marriage after miscarriage?

Annie and Dan's story

The birth of our oldest child fifteen months into our marriage left me little doubt we would be surrounded by many little feet. When she turned one, we wondered. When she turned two, we worried. For years we tried, hoped, prayed, and sought answers. We were told that I was getting older (at twenty-six); we were told to relax.

After trying to conceive our second child for about four years, we lost the baby in an ectopic rupture at six weeks. The trauma of blood loss and emergency surgery were so overwhelming that it took several days to absorb the loss of the pregnancy as the loss of a child. It wasn't until a friend stopped by with a casserole and asked how I was feeling that I really began to process the loss.

The weight of years of secondary infertility, combined with the loss of our second child, hit our marriage hard. I remember one moment in a fight over something so small that I thought, "This is how you break a marriage. I can get up and talk, or I can let this break." So I got up and imperfectly tried.

After losing our baby, we had this empty space in our lives that didn't feel like it belonged to our pursuit of biological children. After a year of licensing and classes, we brought home a newborn foster daughter. Four weeks later, we discovered I was pregnant with our rainbow baby, and we entered the craziest, happiest, busiest two years of our lives.

When our foster daughter was two, her birth father was found. We spent the next six months slowly and agonizingly saying goodbye to the child we had hoped to call our own. In the depths of despair, a friend passed on a referral that brought light and hope with a new doctor, new testing, and answers. We finally learned about reasons and causes for our eight years of secondary infertility.

Once our infertility became a marathon rather than a sprint, we had to pace ourselves. Early in our infertility, there was anxiety and a sense of needing to rush. Slowly, that sense of urgency was replaced with a pace of life that incorporates the possibility of children without that manic rush towards them.

After more than a decade of secondary infertility and two confirmed miscarriages, loss and grief are a tangible part of our marriage. They intertwine in our daily life like a private liturgical calendar. Due dates and loss dates pepper the calendar. New cycles come without the gift of a new life. Medications, timed intercourse, and supplements weigh the daily checklist.

Sometimes my prayer life feels like a dead microphone: I'm talking, but there's no effect. Other times a moment of sheer grace will strike, or the Holy Spirit will place something on my heart so firmly that I know it to be true, even when I don't understand how.

I can think of two particular instances of grace. The first happened in a time of intense spiritual dryness. I had been attending Mass and praying for months with all the vigor of a dried apricot. One Sunday I was sitting in a talk by a sister on our daughterhood in God. Suddenly I was surrounded in complete grace, and I knew we would have five children. With two children in heaven, two on earth, two foster daughters out in the world somewhere and a few suspected early losses, I don't understand how this will be true. But when I think of that moment of complete certainty and grace, I know it to be true. I have peace in knowing I may not understand until heaven.

The second moment came recently. I was falling asleep, worrying about our open foster placements and empty womb and praying for peace. The next morning, I heard the Holy Spirit call, "Boy, boy!" Disoriented and confused, I startled awake, looking for the boys. Then absolute peace settled on my heart. "Ah," I thought, "they're coming." How, when, and where are all uncertain, but our God is a faithful God. So I wait in joyful expectation. On the days that hurt more, in the cycles that break my heart open a little further, I cling to Jeremiah 29:11. God has good plans for us. He will bring us hope for the future.

We have spent the last two years slowly unraveling all of the underlying causes of our secondary infertility. Now we wait, hope, and pray that someday this may all be resolved. As we wait, I strive to find the joy in today, to appreciate the compassion and depth of character that this wait has given me. I strive to seek the light in this darkness, to be the light in someone else's darkness, and to wait in faith that this cross will be my greatest life's work.

Part III

Family, Friends, and the Church

CHAPTER 7

Your Friends and Family

"Blessed be the God and Father of our Lord Jesus Christ,
the Father of compassion and God of all encouragement,
who encourages us in our every affliction, so that we may
be able to encourage those who are in any affliction with the
encouragement with which we ourselves are encouraged by God.
For as Christ's sufferings overflow to us, so through Christ does
our encouragement also overflow." (2 Cor 1:3–5)

Miscarriage may be the most tragic or traumatic loss you have faced thus far. You might feel resentful or depressed; you may be struggling with your faith or in your marriage. You likely do not want to hear anyone else's opinion on your situation or your grief. But you still have to interact with others and go about your daily life. Well-meaning friends and family with deep faith and best intentions may urge you to trust God's plan, offer it up, or remember that God is still good. While each of these truths may eventually help in your healing, you may not be ready to hear them where you are today. How can you handle unintentionally hurtful statements that people make while trying to offer comfort?

All of us have struggled to find the words to speak to someone after their loved one has died. It is difficult for people to see another in pain, especially someone they love. So it is understandable that those around you may want to move you toward resolution. Grief makes many uncomfortable. They may urge you to "get over it" or "move on." Criticisms of grief tend to fall on either end of the spectrum: either you are grieving too much (too publicly or too long) or you are not grieving enough (too stoic or too withdrawn). But mourning has no fixed timeline, and grief is not a problem to be solved; it is a natural response to loss, born out of love.

This chapter will explore the pain and the power of talking about miscarriage with family and friends. Many couples eventually experience a moment of connection or comfort in sharing about their loss, even with a stranger. They often describe being surprised by stories of miscarriage or loss from relatives or friends. This consolation can be a way that God works through our sufferings to bring about encouragement for us and for others.

Suggestions for dealing with others

1. Take care of yourself.
In the early days after miscarriage, you need to tend to your own grief more than worrying about others' feelings. Remember that the way you feel today is not the way you will feel forever. Emotions, even the most intense responses of grief, are never permanent. As time goes on, you may find that you are able to grow in generosity toward others' words or actions. God will be at work in your heart in ways that you cannot see or understand right now. But caring for yourself is a loving act, too.

2. Guard your heart.
You do not need to share your grief with anyone. Grief is intensely personal, and you may wish to grieve privately. A key question to ask yourself, especially in conversation with strangers, is "What part of my story do I want to share with this person, at this time?" The answer may vary from day to day or situation to situation. You may find that opening up to a friend or stranger can bring an unexpected

and healing connection. But you also don't need to tell your whole history to everyone who asks how many kids you have.

3. Prepare in advance.
Practice how you might respond to common questions ("How many kids do you have?" "Weren't you pregnant?" "Are you trying again?"). Ask your spouse how they respond to these questions. Consider answers that are honest about your own experience and compassionate toward the other person. But know that you don't have to stick to the same script every time. Give yourself permission to change your mind in the moment or to excuse yourself and leave a difficult situation.

4. Practice forgiveness.
Pray for a merciful heart. There may always be words that sting. Ultimately, we cannot fault others entirely if their responses are hurtful, because only God's love can be perfect. Remember that people are rarely trying to be intentionally cruel or insensitive. As time goes on, your resilience

"Pray for a merciful heart."

can deepen toward people's unintentionally hurtful words, and you may grow in your compassion for others who are grieving so that you can minister to them out of your experience.

Common responses to miscarriage
In an effort to offer consolation, people often turn to clichés. Clichés usually contain a kernel of truth, but their flaws and limitations can add to the pain of those they hope to comfort. The suggestions below offer new perspectives on clichés commonly spoken to those who are grieving.

Sayings about God
"It's God's will. God has a plan. Everything happens for a reason."

What people mean: Variations on this theological theme rank among the most common responses to miscarriage. People want to set the present suffering within a wider view of the goodness of God's will and the beauty of God's plan for humanity. They also hope to encourage those grieving with the comfort of God's love. But reminding someone who is in pain that "God is good, all the time!" can feel like slapping a band aid on a gaping wound. Parents who are grieving often feel that their pain is dismissed when someone seems to suggest that God wanted or willed the loss of their baby.

What you can remember: God does not desire the death of a child. (See chapter 8 for more on the Church's teaching about God's will.) But within God's loving purposes — for humanity as a whole and for each human life — God can always bring about good from and through suffering. Ultimately God's plan involves the destruction of death and grief at the end of time (as seen in Is 65:19–20 and Rv 21:4).

"God needed another angel. Now your baby is in a better place."

What people mean: When a baby dies, people want to assure grieving parents that their precious child is special in God's eyes, too. The idea that babies would become angels springs from people's desire to envision babies as happy in heaven, but also watching over their parents' lives in a unique way. Yet even the goodness of heaven cannot always ease the natural longing of parents for their child to be here and in their arms.

What you can remember: People do not turn into angels. As the Catholic Church teaches, angels were created all at once at the dawn of time. But instead of becoming angels, humans can become powerful intercessors in eternity, praying for the needs of those still on earth. The Catholic belief in the communion of saints provides deep comfort that we can remain forever connected to those who have died. (See chapter 8 for more on these teachings.)

"Let go and let God. God doesn't give you more than you can handle."

What people mean: Christians often want to encourage each other that God loves and cares for them, and that they can survive difficulties because God will give them strength to endure. While these expressions of concern are based in the truth of God's compassion, such sayings reduce the mystery of God's action in our lives to "cute" clichés more suited to daily irritations or frustrations than the overwhelming depth of grief.

What you can remember: Turning to ancient truth from Scripture may be more comforting than these popular sayings. "The LORD is close to the brokenhearted" (Ps 34:19) and "Jesus wept" (Jn 11:35) remind us that God grieves with the grieving and comforts those who mourn.

Sayings about miscarriage
"At least you can get pregnant. At least it was early."

What people mean: "At least" statements are ironically among the most unhelpful comments made to those who are suffering. While they often spring from a positive belief in the importance of gratitude, these sayings minimize the person's suffering, silencing them from voicing their pain or making them feel like they shouldn't be grieving. "At least you're young." "At least you have other kids." "At least you didn't know the baby."

What you can remember: Research on miscarriage and emotional health has shown that the length of the pregnancy does not determine the extent of the parents' grief. Even the earliest loss can be experienced as devastating, because the parents have already begun to love this baby and imagine a whole life with their child. No one else's perspective on your situation should determine your right to grieve. While gratitude can help in healing, finding your own reasons to be grateful is usually more helpful than being given them by others.

"Something was wrong with the baby; it's for the best. This is nature's way."

What people mean: While it is generally unhelpful to theorize about the cause of a miscarriage, people resort to such explanations because they hope to free you from guilt (i.e., "It wasn't your fault"). These instincts often spring from a place of love, wanting to protect you from pain by putting distance between you and the miscarriage. But rare is the parent who could see the death of their child as "for the best," when this loss is likely experienced as one of the worst griefs imaginable.

What you can remember: The majority of miscarriages are caused by underlying chromosomal issues and have nothing to do with the mother's behavior. But this truth need not lessen your sadness over your loss. You love your baby and will never forget your child. You do not need to "accept" their death under anyone else's terms, and you can seek comfort in the God of love who weeps with the weeping and will one day destroy death forever.

"You can try again. You'll have another."

What people mean: There is hope beyond this present suffering. Miscarriage does not have to define you forever or prevent you from parenting a living child someday. But well-meaning comforters can be too quick to push couples to conceive again. Taking time to mourn this baby means that you may not be ready to think about another child yet. First you can focus on healing, and then you can look ahead to what may come next.

What you can remember: You will forever be the parent of this particular child, this unique soul. Future children cannot replace this baby. And as you now know too well, there are no guarantees in any pregnancy. But rather than trying to predict the future, you can choose to pray for hope and trust in God's mercy and loving plan for your life.

Sayings about grief
"I know exactly how you feel."

What people mean: Because they don't want you to feel alone in grief, people will often try to offer solidarity in your suffering. This attempt to connect might feel comforting if their experience is actually similar to your own (i.e., they lost a baby) or upsetting if their loss doesn't seem to compare at all (i.e., their dog died). But such sayings usually spring from a desire to empathize and draw you out of the darkness of feeling alone in grief.

What you can remember: You are not alone in your pain. Even if the person speaking these words does not understand exactly how you feel, many other parents have suffered the heartache of losing a baby. Seeking out and connecting with those who do share your grief can be a huge source of comfort, and can allow you to accept others' sympathy with greater compassion.

"I can't believe this is happening to you. I can't imagine."

What people mean: Sometimes people are so overwhelmed by another's pain that they try to distance themselves from it (the opposite of "I know exactly how you feel"). They may feel they are honoring your suffering by placing it on a pedestal or not trying to compare it to anything they have experienced. But grieving parents often say these expressions make them feel alienated — that their life is unimaginable to others.

What you can remember: You do have the power to imagine. The root of compassion is found in our ability to imagine. Once we start to picture what it might be like to stand in another's shoes, we can start to "suffer with" them (the meaning of the word "compassion") and let our hearts be moved with love for them. Right now you may have to extend your own imagination to give the benefit of the doubt to those who are trying to comfort you. Later you will likely find that your imagination helps you to empathize with those around you who are hurting.

"Be strong. Time heals all wounds."

What people mean: Clichés of certainty abound in the face of struggle. "Every cloud has a silver lining." "When life gives you lemons, make lemonade." We want to encourage one another in our suffering, which is a beautiful — and deeply Christian — instinct. But we cannot coax or coach one another through pain as easily as we would desire. Perhaps others do see qualities in you which you cannot see as clearly right now: your strength, your faith, or your ability to overcome adversity. Maybe they have found healing in the passage of time for their own deep hurts. But encouragement about the distant future is not always helpful when you are suffering in the present.

What you can remember: No prescribed time frame will fix your sorrow, and no chosen mindset can overcome suffering. But the passage of time does change our grief, as does our own growth in strength. Yet we should not think ourselves weak or slow if we find that grief remains. God is at work in our weakness (2 Cor 12:9), and it is God — not time or attitude — that binds up our wounds (Ps 147:3).

Suggestions to share with family and friends

There are many positive ways to help and support parents in their grief after loss. You may wish to share the following ideas with family and friends to let them know how to care for you. By our words, actions, and prayers, we can all help to create a more compassionate atmosphere around grief in our families, parishes, and communities. (See Appendix B for a list of ways that parishes can support grieving couples.)

Often the best things to say are the simplest: "I'm so sorry. I love you. I'm here for you. You and your baby will not be forgotten." These four expressions of support are outlined in the four steps below: Acknowledge their pain. Listen with love. Support in practical ways. Remember them.

1. Acknowledge their pain.

Especially in a culture that does not speak about miscarriage, grieving parents need their loss to be validated. Don't be afraid to speak of the baby they lost. You aren't reminding them of their child (since they could never have forgotten); you are reminding them that their child is remembered.

- **Send a card**: A sympathy card can mean even more than a phone call, email, or text, since it gives something to hold and keep.
- **Offer a donation**: A memorial gift to a charity related to the baby's loss or a favorite organization is a wonderful way to honor a baby's memory.
- **Give a gift**: Create a care package for the parents (for example, a candle, prayer card, favorite tea or coffee, prayer shawl, journal, or book). Remember their baby with a plant or tree, memorial garden stone, jewelry with the baby's birthstone, picture frame, or a gift personalized with the child's name or initial. Having a Mass offered for the child or enrolling their

name in the prayers of a religious community are two other comforting Catholic traditions.

2. Listen with love.

Scripture counsels us to "weep with those who weep" (Rom 12:15). What grieving parents want more than anything is to have their baby back. Since that is impossible, what you can give them is time and space to grieve. Your support and prayers are the most important ways to help a grieving parent. You do not have to do anything elaborate — simply be present to them in their pain and let them know they are not alone.

- **Follow their lead**: Some people may be open about their loss; others may not want to talk about it. Take your cue from them and ask what they need.
- **Listen more than you talk**: Offer love instead of advice. Try not to fix what can't be fixed. Listen to their story, even if they need to tell it many times.
- **Avoid clichés**: No tidy explanation or trite saying can make sense of what happened. For example, switch "I can't imagine" to "I can only imagine" to extend your empathy. Instead of worrying what to say, just try: "I love you. I'm here for you."

3. Support in practical ways.

Instead of asking how you can help, make a concrete offer. "What can I do?" is often too hard for the bereaved to answer in the fog of grief. In the immediate aftermath of miscarriage, grieving parents need help with life's most basic needs. Offer to buy groceries, help clean the house, mow the lawn, or shovel the driveway. Keep showing up over time.

- **Food**: If you're local, bring a meal or help set up a meal train for others who want to help. If you're long-distance, you can send a gift card for a restaurant, pizza, or groceries, or call a local restaurant to have dinner delivered.
- **Expenses**: Medical bills for any kind of loss — even an early miscarriage — pile up quickly, and burial expenses can be

overwhelming. Even a small financial gift can help a couple burdened by unexpected expenses.

- **Child care**: If the parents have other children, offer to watch the kids for a few hours during the day (so they can rest) or in the evening (so they can get out of the house).

4. Remember them.

Reassure the grieving that you will be with them for the long haul. Call in a week; check in after a month. Be sensitive to how the parents may react to pregnancy news, baby showers, and birth announcements. Don't assume that the couple is "done" grieving after a certain amount of time or after they go on to conceive again.

- **Remember their child**: Set a reminder in your calendar for the day that they lost their baby and reach out to them on the anniversary. Include their baby when you count children or grandchildren, nieces and nephews.
- **Remember the holidays**: Send a note to the parents on Mother's Day and Father's Day — difficult days after the loss of a child. Light a candle at your holiday table to include loved ones who have died. Mention the baby's name in prayer before a special meal. Honor their child with a Christmas ornament or other keepsake.
- **Remember the father**: Don't assume that dad is not grieving as much as mom. Studies show that men are equally affected by miscarriage and that their grief is often unresolved because it goes unacknowledged and unsupported by friends, family, and society.

REFLECTION QUESTIONS

What have people done or said to you that was helpful or hopeful?

What have people said that was hurtful? How do you wish you could have responded?

Jamie and Billy's story

Billy and I were married after dating for over seven years. During that long courtship, we waited until marriage to give ourselves fully to each other. Honestly, I expected to be rewarded with lots of children for waiting so long. But I have been taught to have patience, faith, and trust in God's plan, even if it seems unfair.

We were taught the Billings method of Natural Family Planning during marriage preparation, and we decided to wait six months before trying to conceive our first child. I naively thought that having children would be so easy that we would have to keep track carefully so we didn't have too many surprises.

After about a year, we still were not pregnant. I started to worry that something was wrong. We learned about NaPro Technology, and the nearest NaPro doctor diagnosed a luteal phase defect. On my first round with Clomid we got pregnant, and we were so excited. We decided we would tell our families a few weeks later. After a week of pure bliss, I woke up one night and found blood. I was worried and went to a local lab to have tests done. My HCG numbers had dropped. We were devastated. It was so hard to tell our parents, because we hadn't even had the chance to tell them we were pregnant.

Our first child was almost six weeks along when we lost him or her. It took my body three weeks to fully miscarry. Our loss was so early that for the longest time I was ashamed that I had no remains to bury and no real evidence that our child existed. For months we floundered in a sea of despair. After much thought and prayer, we decided to name our little saint Jesse, which means "gift." We choose to see our child as a gift from God, even if we have to wait until heaven to fully enjoy our little saint.

After much prayer and discussion with our NaPro doctor, we decided to try again. Our first child was never far from our minds. As the months went by, we realized there was something still not right about our fertility. We discovered that my progesterone and estrogen drop too quickly after ovulation, and Billy had low sperm morphology. Our doctor explained we could still get pregnant, but it would take longer since our bodies would both have to be at their best at the same time.

At an appointment with a new NaPro doctor, we found that amazingly, we were pregnant again. The doctor prescribed progesterone shots to maintain the pregnancy. We were overjoyed and expected that this child would survive. But we lost our second child a week later, only days before Christmas. To say we were sad would be a huge understatement. Once again I was sad that my baby was so young (less than five weeks) that I didn't have anything to bury. We also had to get through Christmas: pack away the gifts we planned as announcements and remember the baby in a manger. I was jealous of Mary and every other woman who had been blessed to bring a child into this world. We decided to name our second child Jordan, which means "to descend or flow." I like to think about Jordan's love and prayers flowing down over us as we struggle.

I am an engineer and problem-solver by nature, so my method of coping was to try and discover what part of me was still broken. After months of grieving, we met again with our doctor and learned that I have subclinical hypothyroidism and a gluten sensitivity. I was still hopeful that I could "fix" my body and have healthy babies. This hope and prayer helped us get through our days as a couple with no earthly children. We were still not open about our struggles and sometimes felt judged by large families who assumed that we didn't want children. I am now thirty-six, and most of my friends are celebrating children's birthday parties and spending time with other moms. It is lonely missing children who should be here.

I joined a Facebook group for Catholic women after miscarriage or infant loss. This group has been a gift from God. Suddenly I had so many women who could laugh and cry with me. My loneliness has subsided as I have prayed for these ladies while they pray for me. The importance of such a community cannot be overstated. My husband and I continued to try for our third child, but this time I felt like we had a whole room of people rooting for us. I became better at talking about our children in "real" life, too.

As Mother's Day approached, I became discouraged, dreading the day every year when I want to scream at the world that I am a mother. The day before Mother's Day, my niece gave me a single red rose. It was beautiful but we didn't get home until late and my rose was droopy. I put it in water, but on the morning of Mother's Day it looked even worse — just like how defeated I felt. We went to church where I tried not to be noticed with tears in my eyes. I begged my two saints to show me some sign that they were thinking of me. When we got home, our miracle rose was now standing straight up.

Two days after Mother's Day, we discovered that we were pregnant. We enjoyed a few days of cautious excitement. The rose stayed straight and beautiful throughout the week, which was a blessing — even as I miscarried. We named our third child Austin, which means "great or venerable" or "to increase." I know that this child is great in God's eyes, even if most of the world doesn't know he or she existed. My love for this child has increased my capacity to understand longing and patience.

After losing our third child, my husband was as sad as I was. He was also worried about me. I was feeling broken as a woman, having put myself through so many tests and taken so many vitamins, hormones, and medicines. He asked if we should stop trying because it was so much to deal with each time we experienced a loss. He was struggling that he couldn't protect me from this burden. I didn't know how to comfort him or convince him that we should keep trying regardless of the heartache. That's when he got his own miracle.

Not too long after our third loss, my husband was doing laundry. Upon opening the dryer, he found his Saint Gianna medal sitting right on top of his load of freshly dried T-shirts — the medal he had lost a year earlier. He needed encouragement, and I believe that Saint Gianna and our children provided that little miracle for him. We have taken this miracle as a sign that we should keep trying and trust in God. It does not mean that we will ever have a successful pregnancy, but it is enough to have hope.

Most men and women grieve differently, and this is no exception for us, though we have gotten "better" at grieving together with time and multiple losses. After our first loss I cried a lot, and my husband tried to be the strong one. But I often caught him silently crying over our loss and my despair. After our second miscarriage, he was more open with me about his needs. We both came to understand that while more knowledge of my body and cycles was helpful for me, the information was putting too much stress on him. I found the online group of women where I could express myself without making things worse for him.

I have been through all the stages of grief multiple times. Sometimes I have been angry at God. Why me? Why us? I would be a great mother — why have I not been given the chance? Through prayer, my answer from God seems to be, "Why not you?" This is not heaven. If it were, there would be no sin, sadness, or grief. Everyone's children would be happy and healthy. But I feel like God has placed this burden on us so that we can gain compassion and longing for eternal life. Before these losses, I thought of heaven as a far-off place in distance and time, but now I find myself drawn to heaven — not only because of my own children, but all the children not missed as much as mine.

While I still get frustrated with God's plans and timing, I have made the decision to trust him. I struggle with what it means to be a Catholic woman with no visible children. I am happy to belong to a church family that values all life, but I sometimes feel judged by women who don't know my story and might make assumptions about my openness to starting a family. There is no easy answer when someone asks the dreaded question, "So when are you two going to have kids?" The best answer I have is "I guess that's up to God." If I know them better, I tell them that I have three in heaven and it's not for lack of trying. I want to say that it's none of their business, but I know most people ask out of curiosity and innocence. One of the few positive side effects of miscarriage is that I am more compassionate than before. It is easier to remember that other people may be carrying burdens when I know that I am carrying my own quiet cross.

My husband and I love each other very much, and it is our care for each other's grieving process and needs that has helped us get through these trying times of miscarriage and infertility. When we lean on God and each other, we can get through anything. Time, prayer, and experience have taught us that we still matter as a couple, even without children.

Chapter 8

Wisdom from the Church

"He will destroy death forever.
The Lord God will wipe away
the tears from all faces." (Is 25:8)

Parents who have lost babies to miscarriage often have many questions about their child's fate, the will of God, and eternal life. Such questions have been asked by faithful Christians for centuries. They speak from the heart of what it means to be human. While there are no simple answers for these complex and challenging questions, the Church is the perfect place to grapple with the deepest mysteries of faith.

The Catholic Church affirms the dignity of every human life from the moment of conception and believes in the uniqueness of each soul. So the Church understands and honors the grief of those who mourn. As part of the Body of Christ, this sorrow cannot be ignored, for "If [one] part suffers, all the parts suffer with it" (1 Cor 12:26).

Ultimately the Church seeks to comfort those who mourn and to lead all people to the light of faith in God's goodness.

This chapter gathers the theological wisdom of the Church to speak to questions asked by grieving parents, drawing from Scripture and the *Catechism of the Catholic Church*. No single answer or chapter can sum up Church teaching on matters as complex as salvation and suffering, so we encourage you to bring your own questions to a trusted priest. As lifelong Catholics, we were steeped in the tradition of the Church but did not encounter many of these particular teachings until life brought us here. Over time the hope and promise of these teachings has brought us comfort and deepened our faith that God continues to care for our children. We join with you in praying for an increase in wisdom to live with the mysteries of what cannot be understood fully in this life.

Is our baby in heaven? What if our baby wasn't baptized?

The *Catechism* speaks straight to this most urgent and heartfelt question asked by parents of babies who were miscarried: "As regards children who have died without Baptism, the Church can only entrust them to the mercy of God, as she does in her funeral rites for them. Indeed, the great mercy of God who desires that all men should be saved, and Jesus' tenderness toward children which caused him to say: 'Let the children come to me, do not hinder them,' allow us to hope that there is a way of salvation for children who have died without Baptism" (CCC 1261). These words call us to deep and abiding hope, trusting in God's mercy and compassion for each human soul.

The question of what happens to unbaptized babies has been a theological debate from the earliest days of the Church, as theologians and Church leaders sought to explain and defend the importance of baptism. Over time the concept of limbo was developed in response to this question: a state that was neither heaven nor hell, but a place for the souls of babies who die without baptism. However, limbo was never an officially defined Catholic doctrine and is not mentioned in the *Catechism of the Catholic Church*: "This theory, elaborated by theologians beginning in the Middle Ages, never entered into the dogmatic definitions of the Magisterium, even if that same

Magisterium did at times mention the theory in its ordinary teaching up until the Second Vatican Council."[2]

The Church has recently reexamined the traditional teaching surrounding limbo. In 2007 the Vatican International Theological Commission published "The Hope of Salvation for Infants who Die without Being Baptised," a study begun at the request of Pope Saint John Paul II and released under Pope Benedict XVI. The document addresses this question directly and compassionately. (See Appendix D for the link to the full text.)

> Our conclusion is that the many factors that we have considered above give serious theological and liturgical grounds for hope that unbaptised (*sic*) infants who die will be saved and enjoy the Beatific Vision. We emphasise (*sic*) that these are reasons for prayerful *hope*, rather than grounds for sure knowledge. There is much that simply has not been revealed to us (cf. Jn 16:12). We live by faith and hope in the God of mercy and love who has been revealed to us in Christ, and the Spirit moves us to pray in constant thankfulness and joy (cf. 1 Thess 5:18). What has been revealed to us is that the ordinary way of salvation is by the sacrament of Baptism. None of the above considerations should be taken as qualifying the necessity of Baptism or justifying delay in administering the sacrament. Rather, as we want to reaffirm in conclusion, they provide strong grounds for hope that God will save infants when we have not been able to do for them what we would have wished to do, namely, to baptize them into the faith and life of the Church.[3]

The Church upholds the importance of baptism for salvation but also teaches that baptism is a sacrament for the living and that God's saving power is not limited by the sacraments: "Baptism is necessary for salvation for those to whom the Gospel has been proclaimed and

---

2. International Theological Commission, *The Hope of Salvation for Infants who Die without Being Baptized*, introductory material.

3. Paragraphs 102–103, emphasis in original.

who have had the possibility of asking for this sacrament.... God has bound salvation to the sacrament of Baptism, but he himself is not bound by his sacraments" (CCC 1257). In citing this teaching from the *Catechism*, the 2007 Vatican document explains that "God can therefore give the grace of Baptism without the sacrament being conferred, and this fact should particularly be recalled when the conferring of Baptism would be impossible. The need for the sacrament is not absolute."[4]

As grieving parents, this belief that God can give grace outside the sacraments has brought us great comfort. While we could not baptize our baby who was miscarried (since this child had died before birth), we felt peace even in our grief that our child was back in the hands of God. Yet our experience of not being able to give that baby the gift of baptism also affirmed for us the importance of the sacrament. Years later, once we learned of the rare complication that our twins had developed in utero, this belief in the centrality of baptism was the reason we knew we wanted to have them baptized as soon as possible. Franco baptized our daughters in the hospital NICU right after their birth — a gift that he could give them as their father and a connection to the legacy of their sibling's life. We have great hope that our children are in heaven with God. This hope has deepened our awe and wonder at the mystery of eternal life: to believe that our children are waiting there for us and that they are still living, beyond what we can see or know.

Ultimately, the Church calls us not to despair but to pray for our beloved babies and to entrust all our lives to the mercy of God who created and loves us. Words from the funeral rite gather this hope, faith, and trust into one beautiful prayer: "Dear friends, in the face of death all human wisdom fails. Yet the Lord teaches us, by the three days he spent in the tomb, that death has no hold over us. Christ has conquered death; his dying and rising have redeemed us. Even in our sorrow for the loss of this little child, we believe that, one short sleep past, he/she will wake eternally."[5]

---

4. "The Hope of Salvation," no. 82.

5. *Order of Christian Funerals,* Rite of Final Commendation for An Infant, no. 337. Excerpt from the English translation of *Order of Christian Funerals* ©1985, 1989, International Commission on English in the Liturgy Corporation. All rights reserved.

Is our baby an angel? A saint?

Each time we lost a child, whether before or after birth, we knew that our babies did not become angels. Yet people often referred to our babies as angels — for instance, "God needed another angel" or "now you have a special guardian angel watching over you." Parents we met in grief support groups frequently used the term "angel baby" to refer to their baby who had died. Angel wings are commonly found on sympathy cards, memorial ornaments, and children's gravestones. While we knew that those who used this term wanted to express love for our babies or assure us that they remained connected to our lives in a special way, we understood that the Catholic faith has a different teaching about what happens to us when we die.

The Church teaches that angels are purely spiritual beings, special servants and messengers of God "present since creation" (CCC 328–333). Human beings are different kinds of creatures, with bodies and souls. We do not turn into angels when we die. Instead, our souls go to God while our physical bodies await the resurrection of the dead when Christ will come again at the end of time: "In death, the separation of the soul from the body, the human body decays and the soul goes to meet God, while awaiting its reunion with its glorified body. God, in his almighty power, will definitively grant incorruptible life to our bodies by reuniting them with our souls, through the power of Jesus' Resurrection" (CCC 997). For those of us who long for children we never got to hold, we can draw great hope from the possibility of being able to see,

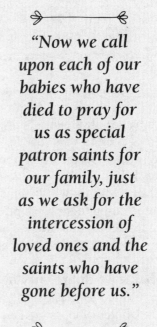

"Now we call upon each of our babies who have died to pray for us as special patron saints for our family, just as we ask for the intercession of loved ones and the saints who have gone before us."

touch, and hold our children in heaven, in whatever form this will take in our glorified bodies.

Instead of becoming angels, those who have died remain part of the communion of saints, which is the united body of believers on earth, in purgatory, and in heaven. The Church's teaching on the communion of saints means that those who have gone before us can now intercede to God on our behalf (CCC 962). Just as we ask canonized saints to pray for us to God, we can also ask our children who have died to pray for us and others, while we pray for them in turn: "Our prayer for them [those who have died] is capable not only of helping them, but also of making their intercession for us effective" (CCC 958).

The idea that our children could be "little saints" truthfully felt foreign to us when we first heard the term from fellow Catholics. This language was not an expression or concept that we had grown up hearing. But it affirmed our belief in the communion of saints and our own call to holiness. Now we call upon each of our babies who have died to pray for us as special patron saints for our family, just as we ask for the intercession of loved ones and the saints who have gone before us. The thought of our children interceding for us is a powerful comfort, uniting them to us forever within the communion of saints.

The promise of eternal life means that those who have died are still living, beyond what we can grasp by the limits of our senses. Death ends physical life here on earth, but it does not end life — and it does not end your love for your child. Saint Simeon of Thessalonica offers hopeful words about our connection to those who have gone before us: "For even dead, we are not at all separated from one another, because we all run the same course and we will find one another again in the same place. We shall never be separated, for we live for Christ, and now we are united with Christ as we go toward him ... we shall all be together in Christ" (quoted in CCC 1690).

What if we didn't bury our baby?

The Church teaches that burial is a final act of care for the person: "The Church who, as Mother, has borne the Christian sacramentally in her womb during his earthly pilgrimage, accompanies him at his journey's end, in order to surrender him 'into the Father's hands.' She offers to the Father, in Christ, the child of his grace, and she commits to the earth, in hope, the seed of the body that will rise in glory" (CCC 1683). As humans were made from dust, so our bodies return to the earth waiting in hope to be raised again: "And the dust returns to the earth as it once was, and the life breath returns to God who gave it" (Eccl 12:7).

But many parents who experience miscarriage, especially early in pregnancy, may not have been able to find or keep the remains of their baby. This can lead to guilt about not being able to care for their child's body as they wished. It is important to remember that miscarriage is a terrible suffering for which parents cannot plan or prepare fully. The official prayers and rites available to parents after a miscarriage, even if the baby's body is not present, can provide comfort in the knowledge that the Church still blesses this child (see chapter 9).

Scripture reminds us, too, that God is the Lord of the living and the dead: "For if we live, we live for the Lord, and if we die, we die for the Lord; so then, whether we live or die, we are the Lord's. For this is why Christ died and came to life, that he might be Lord of both the dead and the living" (Rom 14:7–9). No matter how you were ultimately able to care for your child's body after miscarriage, your baby remains a beloved child of God.

When Laura miscarried at home, we had no idea that the remains could be collected for burial. So we were not able to bury this child. Yet we later found comfort in visiting a nearby Catholic cemetery with a special monument for miscarried babies in the children's section. Knowing that other parents shared this same sacred space as a place of memorial for their babies, whether or not they were buried there, brought us peace. When our daughters died after birth, we had their remains cremated and buried in this same cemetery. Being able to celebrate the beautiful Rite of Committal at their grave, to return their bodies to the earth, and to allow the Christian community to pray for them has been deeply meaningful for us. If you were able to have your child's remains cremated but have not yet buried them, you can always ask a priest to celebrate the Final Committal to bury the body at a later date. Affirming the goodness of human bodies as created by God, the Church teaches that cremated remains should be buried, instead of popular practices like sprinkling ashes, keeping funerary urns at home, or collecting the remains within memorial jewelry or other keepsakes. (See Appendix D for more information on the 2016 Vatican document that addresses burial after cremation.) The act of placing your baby's remains within a cemetery or columbarium allows the Body of Christ to remember your baby with you and to unite their prayers with yours.

Why did God let this happen? Is this part of God's plan?

As Christians we believe that God, who is all-powerful, all-knowing, all-loving, and all-merciful, is in control of our lives. The doctrine of providence describes God's plan for creation: God desires good for all his creatures and is actively involved in each human life. But even in light of God's providence, Christians have always wrestled with questions of suffering and death. How could a loving God allow people to suffer? Why wouldn't an all-knowing and all-powerful God prevent bad things from happening?

We asked all of these questions after our miscarriage. As a couple, we have found great comfort in learning how Scripture teaches that God does not desire death and that the deaths of these little ones would never have been part of the perfect plan of God's love for us. Learning about the difference between God's perfect will and permissive will helped us to come to a deeper understanding of God's role in suffering and death. God's perfect (or active) will was the original plan for all of creation, which always desires only good for each one of us. God's permissive will is what God allows to happen. God never directly wills evil. But because God gave humans free will — the freedom to choose good or to choose sin — and because humans chose sin, the consequences of sin include suffering and death.

Death was not part of God's original plan for humanity: "Even though man's nature is mortal, God had destined him not to die. Death was therefore contrary to the plans of God the Creator and entered the world as a consequence of sin. 'Bodily death, from which man would have been immune had he not sinned' is thus 'the last enemy' of man left to be conquered" (CCC 1008). Scripture insists that God did not create death nor does God desire the death of his beloved creatures:

- "Because God did not make death, nor does he rejoice in the destruction of the living. For he fashioned all things that they might have being." (Wis 1:13–14)
- "He does not willingly afflict or bring grief to human beings." (Lam 3:33)
- "The last enemy to be destroyed is death." (1 Cor 15:26)

But the Church also teaches that death has been conquered by Christ, who suffered and died to transform "the curse of death into a blessing" (CCC 1009). God can bring good out of evil, thus redeeming suffering: "By his passion and death on the cross Christ has given a new meaning to suffering: it can henceforth configure us to him and unite us with his redemptive Passion" (CCC 1505). We are called to trust that God, through his permissive will, is always at work to bring good out of suffering. As we mourn our children, we can unite ourselves with all who are suffering and ask God to work through our pain to bring about healing, hope, and new life.

The death of your baby has likely ushered you into a new understanding of the reality of suffering throughout the world. The Church acknowledges how heavy these burdens are for the faithful to bear. But the beauty of being part of a universal Church is knowing that you are never alone in your suffering or your desire for understanding in questions of faith. Uniting yourself in prayer with the Body of Christ can allow you to come to know Christ's own sufferings in a deeper way as you ask God to comfort, enlighten, and strengthen your grieving heart.

Throughout our journey of grief, we have been consoled by a strong sense that God weeps with us and that the heart of God knows the pain of losing a beloved child. We have also come to understand how God works to transform suffering into good and how we are called to let our hearts be more open to the suffering in the world. Ultimately we keep learning to live with the mystery that there are no easy answers or explanations in the face of death. We await in joyful hope the day when we might understand, when we meet God face to face.

REFLECTION QUESTIONS

Which questions of faith have been hardest for you after miscarriage?

Which questions do you want to bring to God in prayer?

Mary Ruth and Bob's story

We lost our second child when I was thirteen weeks along. We had been trying for a few months. It was a difficult winter because I lost both my grandfather and grandmother that year. I loved being pregnant because it was so hopeful for the future. But then I miscarried and lost the baby.

We were on a trip for a friend's wedding. It was a very formal affair, and because of the fit of the gown, it was obvious to everyone I was pregnant. A few nights after announcing the pregnancy, I started bleeding. We were 3,000 miles from home, and it was really scary. Our practitioners were very clinical about the miscarriage, even calling it by its technical term: a "spontaneous abortion." I was repulsed that they could call it that. It felt like such a clear statement that my body had failed in its job to protect and nurture this child.

Because the baby was so small, they gave me the option of taking a pill and miscarrying at home on my own timeline. That was all they said. My mother flew out to be with me. I dropped my son at a friend's house and then popped the pill. It was horrible. No one had prepared me. It was an actual labor. Then at the moment of the actual "delivery," I was utterly alone. They had said I would pass a tissue mass and I should just flush it. It all seemed so clinical. It was heartbreaking.

My friends didn't know how to react. One had actually had an abortion in high school, so there was some tension there. Here I was grieving a child when she had actually chosen to do it to herself. Another friend simply said, "This is a big deal, but I don't know how big of a deal." A third friend sent a beautiful bouquet of flowers. That was the best. She treated it like a life lost. That is what it was.

My husband and I grieved together yet alone. I cried and talked; I made a scrapbook and kept a journal. My husband mostly supported me in whatever I needed to do. He took a supportive role and seemed to heal through supporting my healing. He just wanted me to be better again. It was hard for my husband to understand the depth of loss for me, but he recognized it and recommended that I speak to a priest about it. Knowing that he wanted to help me was comforting. I appreciated (and still do!) his suggestion that we see a priest.

I found great comfort in the Church. I wasn't Catholic at the time, but I was drawn to the Church after losing our daughter because it seemed the only place that her life was not only recognized but really valued. The loss of her life was the catalyst to me both developing a deeper spiritual life and beginning the process of coming into the Church.

We conceived a few months after losing Lily and went on to have three healthy children. We talk about Lily. She is still part of the family. She came before three of our four children, so they have grown up knowing that they have an older sister. God willing, they will meet her someday in heaven. Our oldest doesn't remember that part of our lives, but they all recognize that pregnancies are delicate so we are all careful to pray for our friends who are expecting.

CHAPTER 9

Saints, Prayers, and Support from the Church

"See, I am creating new heavens
and a new earth;
The former things shall not be remembered
nor come to mind.
Instead, shout for joy and be glad forever
in what I am creating.
Indeed, I am creating Jerusalem to be a joy
and its people to be a delight;
I will rejoice in Jerusalem
and exult in my people.
No longer shall the sound of weeping be heard there,
or the sound of crying;
No longer shall there be in it
an infant who lives but a few days,
nor anyone who does not live a full lifetime." (Is 65:17–20)

Grief will be no more when Christ comes again. Until that joyful day when we hope to be reunited in heaven with all those we love, we turn to the Body of Christ here on earth to help comfort us in our suffering. The Church's tradition offers many resources that can give care, support, and hope to grieving parents. This chapter gathers prayers, rites, and saints that speak directly to the grief of losing a baby, as well as ideas for how parishes can reach out to couples after miscarriage.

Official Rites

The *Book of Blessings* includes a "Blessing of Parents after a Miscarriage or Stillbirth" which may be used by a priest, deacon, or lay minister. (The full order of the blessing can be found in Appendix C.) The blessing speaks to the sorrow of parents who have lost a baby and seek God's comfort, strength, and healing. Since the blessing may be offered to parents without the presence of the baby's body, it can be an especially fitting prayer for early miscarriage.

The Church's Funeral Rites for Children also address children who died without baptism: "Funeral rites may be celebrated for children whose parents intended them to be baptized but who died before baptism. In these celebrations the Christian community entrusts the child to God's all-embracing love and finds strength in this love and in Jesus' affirmation that the kingdom of God belongs to little children."[6]

The Church provides special funeral rites for infants with particular prayers for baptized children and babies who died before baptism. These rites include options which can be celebrated in the hospital, family home, church, or funeral home, depending on the situation:

- Vigil for a Deceased Child
- Funeral Liturgy (either within Mass or outside Mass)
- Rite of Committal (celebrated at the grave, tomb, or crematorium)
- Rite of Final Commendation for an Infant (which may be

---

6. *Order of Christian Funerals*, no. 237. Excerpt from the English translation of *Order of Christian Funerals* ©1985, 1989, International Commission on English in the Liturgy Corporation. All rights reserved.

used in the hospital or family home, with or without the presence of the child's body)

These examples of prayers from the funeral rites are beautiful expressions of the Church's hope in eternal life. (See Appendix C for additional prayers from the Funeral Rites for Children.)

OPENING PRAYER FOR FUNERAL MASS[7]
God of all consolation,
searcher of mind and heart,
the faith of these parents *[N. and N.]* is known to you.

Comfort them with the knowledge
that the child for whom they grieve
is entrusted now to your loving care.

We ask this through Christ our Lord.
R/. Amen.

COMMITTAL FROM THE RITE OF COMMITTAL[8]
Lord God,
ever caring and gentle,
we commit to your love this little one *[N.]*,
who brought joy to our lives for so short a time.
Enfold him/her in eternal life.

We pray for his/her parents
who are saddened by the loss of their child [baby/infant].
Give them courage
and help them in their pain and grief.
May they all meet one day
in the joy and peace of your kingdom.
We ask this through Christ our Lord.
R/. Amen.

---

7. *Order of Christian Funerals*, 254 C (A child who died before baptism). Excerpts from the English translation of *Order of Christian Funerals* ©1985, 1989, International Commission on English in the Liturgy Corporation. All rights reserved.
8. *Order of Christian Funerals*, 322 B (A child who died before baptism).

Several U.S. dioceses have published their own naming rites for babies who died before birth. (Check with your diocese for permission to use these prayers.) They can be used whether the baby's body is present or not. Several of the rites are available in full online in booklet form, including "life certificates" to fill out in honor of the child:

- Order for the Naming and Commendation of an Infant Who Died before Birth — Archdiocese of St. Louis
- Ceremony of Naming and Commendation for an Infant Who Died before Birth — Archdiocese of Atlanta
- Naming Ceremony — Diocese of Fargo
- Order for the Naming and Commendation of an Infant Who Died before Birth — Diocese of Wichita

Sacraments and sacramentals

Sacraments can offer profound grace and comfort in your grief. When we long for God in grief, receiving Christ in the Eucharist brings the grace of lasting presence. For mothers who received communion while pregnant, they often find comfort in the thought that their unborn child, who was nourished by every food they ate, could also have been touched by the grace of this sacrament while in the womb. (Chapter 9 describes how the communion of saints — in heaven and on earth — is united in a special way in the celebration of the Mass.)

Depending on the particular circumstances of your miscarriage, especially if surgery or serious complications are involved, you may wish to ask a priest for the Anointing of the Sick. This sacrament is not limited to those who are at the point of death but also in case of "grave illness" (CCC 1514). The Anointing of the Sick can take place in the home, hospital, or church. The Sacrament of Reconciliation can also be a powerful experience of healing if you are carrying guilt, despair, or anger at God about your loss.

For example, our pastor celebrated the Sacrament of the Anointing of the Sick before Laura's surgery when our twin daughters were so sick in-utero. To have this powerful experience of anointing when we were filled with anxiety and fear was a sacred moment of prayer. Later, our oldest son celebrated his first Sacrament of Reconciliation a few months after our twins had died, and in preparing for the sacrament with him, we each had the chance to experience God's healing invitation of forgiveness when we went to confession.

Sacramentals are "sacred signs which bear a resemblance to the sacraments" (CCC 1667) and include popular devotions like the Rosary, pilgrimages, and the Stations of the Cross as well as sacred objects like holy water, religious medals, and saints' relics. These physical objects and prayer practices that remind us of God's abiding presence can be especially meaningful when we are consumed by grief at the absence of the one we love. Many grieving parents have found comfort in wearing a saint's medal that connects to their baby's name or having a rosary made from dried flowers from their child's funeral (available from Catholic vendors online).

> *"These physical objects and prayer practices which remind us of God's abiding presence can be especially meaningful when we are consumed by grief at the absence of the one we love."*

Prayers

Beyond official Church rites, a number of popular prayers can offer comfort to parents who have suffered miscarriages. For Franco, Scripture was the most helpful way to pray after miscarriage. He kept a copy of 2 Corinthians 4:7-11 at his desk at work, and whenever he needed, he could return to these words: "We are afflicted in every way, but not constrained; perplexed, but not driven to despair; persecuted, but not abandoned; struck down, but not destroyed." For Laura, turning to Mary in prayer was invaluable. A friend had gifted a beautiful pink and blue rosary in honor of our baby, and holding something tangible during prayer awakened in Laura a sense of newfound companionship with Mary — as a mother who understood suffering and who had watched her child die.

Mary can offer a profound source of comfort and intercession for grieving parents. Since Mary was present at the death of Jesus, the Church teaches us to pray for her intercession "at the hour of our death" — that she might pray for our own salvation and our peace in the final moments of our lives. Because Mary is a special intercessor for those who are dying, we can know that she also cares in a special way for our babies who have died.

Other popular Marian prayers speak directly to the sorrow and suffering of the faithful. In the Memorare we pray: "To thee do I come, before thee I stand, sinful and sorrowful," a reminder that Mary knows and sees our grief. In the last months of pregnancy with our twins, when we knew they had developed a potentially fatal complication, the Memorare was the most powerful prayer we could return to in moments of fear or despair.

Other parents have found comfort in the words of the Hail Holy Queen, which is prayed as part of the Rosary and includes the line "To thee do we cry, poor banished children of Eve, to thee do we send up our sighs, mourning and weeping in this vale of tears." The Church also prays the Sorrowful Mysteries of the Rosary as a way to meditate on the suffering of Jesus and Mary. You may wish to learn more about particular devotions based on the sufferings endured by Christ and his mother; for example, the Sacred Heart of Jesus, the Immaculate Heart of Mary, Our Lady of Sorrows, and Mary, Undoer of Knots.

Another prayer that has long been meaningful for grieving parents is Mother Angelica's prayer, which invites parents to imagine their baby close to God in heaven. (See Appendix C for more prayers that have been meaningful in times of grief over the loss of a baby.)

My Lord, the baby is dead!

Why, my Lord — dare I ask why? It will not hear the whisper of the wind or see the beauty of its parents' face — it will not see the beauty of Your creation or the flame of a sunrise. Why, my Lord?

"Why, My child — do you ask 'why'? Well, I will tell you why.

You see, the child lives. Instead of the wind he hears the

sound of angels singing before My throne. Instead of the beauty that passes he sees everlasting Beauty — he sees My face. He was created and lived a short time so the image of his parents imprinted on his face may stand before Me as their personal intercessor. He knows secrets of heaven unknown to men on earth. He laughs with a special joy that only the innocent possess. My ways are not the ways of man. I create for My Kingdom and each creature fills a place in that Kingdom that could not be filled by another. He was created for My joy and his parents' merits. He has never seen pain or sin. He has never felt hunger or pain. I breathed a soul into a seed, made it grow and called it forth."[9]

Saints
The Church has many saints whose intercession has touched couples grieving the loss of a child. The following stories, traditional prayers, and attributed quotes from saints may be helpful for your reflection in times of grief.

Saints Anne and Joachim: patron saints of couples suffering from infertility
The United States Conference of Catholic Bishops has published a Novena to Saints Anne and Joachim, the parents of the Blessed Virgin Mary. Tradition holds that after years of childlessness, Saint Joachim went to the desert to pray and fast for forty days in the hopes of having a child. Angels then appeared to both Saint Joachim and Saint Anne, promising them that they would have a child. For this reason, the parents of Mary are "powerful intercessors for all married couples, expectant mothers and married couples who are having difficulty conceiving."[10] (See Appendix A for more information.)

Saint Bernard of Clairvaux
A popular story tells of a couple who had a miscarriage and wrote to Saint Bernard of Clairvaux, asking, "What is going to happen to

---

9.   Mother M. Angelica, "Miscarriage Prayer," EWTN.com; used with permission.

10.   United States Conference of Catholic Bishops, "Saints Anne and Joachim Novena," http://www.usccb.org/issues-and-action/marriage-and-family/natural-family-planning/upload/nfp-sts-anne-joachim-novena.pdf.

my child? The child didn't get baptized." Saint Bernard is said to have responded: "Your faith spoke for this child. Baptism for this child was only delayed by time. Your faith suffices. The waters of your womb — were they not the waters of life for this child? Look at your tears. Are they not like the waters of baptism? Do not fear this. God's ability to love is greater than our fears. Surrender everything to God."

Saint Catherine of Siena: Patron saint of miscarriages
Traditional prayer for the intercession of Saint Catherine of Siena

Humble Virgin and Doctor of the Church,
in thirty-three years
you achieved great perfection
and became the counselor of Popes.
　You know the temptations of mothers today
as well as the dangers that await unborn infants.
　Intercede for me
that I may avoid miscarriage
and bring forth a healthy baby
who will become a true child of God.
　Also pray for all mothers,
that they may not resort to abortion
but help bring a new life into the world. Amen.

Saint Catherine of Sweden: Patron saint of miscarriages
Traditional prayer for the intercession of Saint Catherine of Sweden

Dear Saint Catherine, patron of those who have suffered a miscarriage, you know the dangers that await unborn infants. Please intercede for me that I may receive healing from the loss I have suffered. My soul has been deprived of peace and I have forgotten what true happiness is. As I mourn the loss of my child, I place myself in the hands of God and ask for strength to accept His will in all things, for consolation in my grief, and for peace in my sorrow.

　Glorious Saint Catherine, hear my prayers and ask that God, in good time, grant me a healthy baby who will become a true child of

God. Amen.

Saint Gianna Beretta Molla: Patron saint of mothers and unborn babies

Saint Gianna was an Italian pediatrician who suffered two miscarriages and died from complications following the birth of her fourth child, for whom she chose life rather than an abortion or hysterectomy for a fibroma on her uterus.

"Love and sacrifice are closely linked, like the sun and the light. We cannot love without suffering and we cannot suffer without love."

Saint Gerard Majella: Patron saint of motherhood, childbirth, and unborn children

"Who except God can give you peace? Has the world ever been able to satisfy the heart?"

Saint Elizabeth Ann Seton: Patron saint for the death of a child

"We must often draw the comparison between time and eternity. This is the remedy of all our troubles. How small will the present moment appear when we enter that great ocean."

Saint Joseph: Patron saint of fathers, husbands, and the dying

Prayer to Saint Joseph, Patron of the Unborn[11]

O St. Joseph, after your most holy spouse, our Blessed Mother, you were the first to take into your arms and heart the baby Jesus. From the first time you gazed upon him and held him, your heart and soul were forever bonded to him. You caressed the Holy Child with fatherly love and affection, and you committed yourself always to love, protect, and care for this Son.

Look now with similar love and affection upon this child of mine, who has gone from this world. I place my child, as well as my grief and guilt, into the eternal embrace of your arms. Hold and caress my child for me with the love of my arms and sweetly kiss my child with all the tender affection of my heart.

---

11. Used with permission of the Oblates of St. Joseph, Holy Spouses Province.

As God the Father entrusted the care of His most precious Son into your most loving and confident hands, so too do I entrust into your fatherly care this child of mine. Please present him to the merciful hands of Our Lord, so that one day, when I too leave this world, my child may greet me into eternal life. Amen.

Saints Zélie and Louis Martin: Patron saints of marriage, parenting, and illness

The parents of Saint Thérèse of Lisieux were the first husband and wife to be canonized together. They endured the deaths of four of their nine children in infancy or early childhood.

"When I closed the eyes of my dear little children and when I buried them, I felt great pain, but it was always with resignation. I didn't regret the sorrows and the problems I had endured for them. Several people said to me, 'It would be better to never have had them.' I can't bear that kind of talk. I don't think the sorrows and problems could be weighed against the eternal happiness of my children. So they weren't lost forever. Life is short and full of misery. We'll see them again in Heaven. Above all, it was on the death of my first child that I felt more deeply the happiness of having a child in Heaven, for God showed me in a noticeable way that He accepted my sacrifice. Through the intercession of my little angel, I received a very extraordinary grace." (Saint Zélie Martin in Letter 72)[12]

REFLECTION QUESTIONS

When has God felt most present (or absent) to you in your grief?

What prayers, Scripture, saints, or sacraments have been comforting to you?

---

12. Zélie and Louis Martin, *A Call to a Deeper Love: The Family Correspondence of the Parents of St. Thérèse of the Child Jesus*, 1863–1885 (New York: Society of St. Paul, 2011), 90–91.

Molly and Ben's story

The books prepare you for a loss if you read them closely enough. In that little, unassuming box in the corner they tell you about the chances of miscarriage (one in four), and that it's normal and not to worry because a viable pregnancy will be just around the corner. But that doesn't prepare you to hear the words "empty," or "no heartbeat," or "I'm so sorry; we don't need the room, take your time," over and over again. That little unassuming box in the corner doesn't tell you how to cry silently in a bathroom at work or smile convincingly during baptisms at church. It doesn't tell you how to cope with early ultrasounds, blood draws, and long waits in the bathroom straining to see little pink lines, month after month, year after year.

We never thought we would be part of the miscarriage statistics. We never imagined we would be part of the select few who miscarry repeatedly with no explanation and no cure. For us there were no shots to make it better, no calls to a doctor that would figure it all out. It was just the way the genetic lottery unfolded again and again.

Some months were braver than others. After our first loss it was easy to try again; after all, the books said it was a fluke and we'd be holding our next child again soon. Even after the shock of the second miscarriage, we mourned and moved on quickly, hoping for joy to overshadow would-have-been due dates and milestones. It was after the third loss that things changed.

Our third loss was different. She lived longer than her siblings. We saw her heartbeat and have the tiniest ultrasound picture of her. But because of that her loss was harder. We needed more time to mourn her, to mourn the news of her Trisomy-16 diagnosis, and to deal with the effects it could have on our future attempts to conceive.

After her loss, I declared that I needed a break. I couldn't just jump back in to trying to conceive. One night I told my husband that in the past all I thought about was if I was ready to be pregnant again. But now I knew I couldn't try for another child unless I was prepared also to lose them, too. I had to be ready for birth and death now that I knew how closely the two danced together.

It took over six months. For six months I mourned and raged at my body and sulked at happy families in the park and cried over my oldest child and everything I couldn't give him. We had to learn to trust God — the trust they speak about when they say the Lord gives and takes away. We had to work hard to reconnect to each other through and after the mourning.

We needed time to remember that there were many fruits of a good marriage and the other fruits were also worth cultivating. We needed time to remember our marriage and ourselves were not meant to be used as a means solely to produce more children. We needed time to remember that parenthood has a physical and a spiritual dimension and that we have responsibilities to the other children in our lives — ours and others' — not just the ones we were trying to conceive. The break gave us time to heal ourselves, our bodies, and our marriage, to realign our lives and desires back to God.

After three years of trial and after yet another loss, we visited the Shrine of Our Lady of Guadalupe in Wisconsin. It wasn't the first time we had been there, but it was the first time I went without expectation — not with demands for God, but with acceptance. We stood in front of statues of Mary cradling little babies in her arms and prayed for the little ones we will never hold in this world. We knelt in front of holy relics, and for the first time we didn't pray for children. Instead we prayed for God's will to be done, for trust in his plan and acceptance in our hearts. We prayed for peace in our minds and for his plan for our family.

Nine months later, to the day, our daughter was born.

Part IV

The Future
after Miscarriage

CHAPTER 10

Ways to Remember Your Baby

"Sing out, heavens, and rejoice, earth,
break forth into song, you mountains,
For the Lord comforts his people
and shows mercy to his afflicted.
But Zion said, 'The Lord has forsaken me;
my Lord has forgotten me.'
Can a mother forget her infant,
be without tenderness for the child of her womb?
Even should she forget,
I will never forget you.
See, upon the palms of my hands I have engraved you."
(Is 49:13–16)

You will never forget your baby. Your love for your child is carved on your heart. While it may feel painful at the beginning to think of your loss, remembering your baby in concrete ways — with a keepsake, favorite prayer, or ritual on their anniversary each year —

can help the grieving process. Honoring the life of your child is an important part of healing and helps to keep their memory alive in your daily life.

"How many children do you have?" is a complicated question for parents after miscarriage. No matter how you choose to respond in different situations, this innocent, ordinary question captures the complexities of life after loss: easy answers no longer exist. But you will forever be the parents of this unique child, and you have every right to remember them as you desire.

Keepsakes and mementos

You may decide that you want a visual reminder of your child in your home or workplace: a card with their name or dates, a color that reminds you of your baby, or a Scripture verse that speaks to your grief. Even a small ritual like listening to a favorite song on a difficult day can help you connect to your child.

Grieving parents have shared many ideas for tangible reminders of their babies:

- Journal where you can record memories about your pregnancy (like the day you found out you were expecting or the way you shared the news with family or friends)
- Framed print of a favorite prayer, quote from a saint, Scripture verse, ultrasound photo, or handprints/footprints
- Certificate of Life from the Shrine of the Holy Innocents (see Appendix A)
- For moms: earrings or a necklace with your baby's initials, birthstone, or a charm representing your baby; a locket or mother's ring
- For dads: an ID bracelet or key chain engraved with your child's name, initials, or dates; a pin for your coat or wallet
- Rosary
- Candle
- Prayer card from your baby's patron saint
- Shadow box with a baby hat, onesie, socks, or shoes
- Stuffed animal or bear
- Memorial tattoo

- Christmas ornament or stocking
- Memorial plant, tree, garden, or statue
- Favorite songs that remind you of your baby or pregnancy
- If you were able to record your child's heartbeat, you can convert the recording into a visual canvas or print (search online for options)

If you had an early loss, you may not have an ultrasound photo or footprints. But there are still many ways to remember your baby. You can create a keepsake box of mementos: the positive pregnancy test (or a photo of it), dried flowers, photos taken during your pregnancy (whether "belly shots" or other photos from the time when you were pregnant), sympathy cards, a photo of your baby's name written in the sand or painted on a rock, or a page of a daily prayer book from the day you learned you were expecting or the date of your miscarriage. However you choose to honor your child is a private decision — whatever brings you comfort.

Anniversaries

You likely have several meaningful dates on the calendar, like the day you learned you were expecting, the day of the miscarriage, or the original due date. You might also wish to celebrate your child on the feast day of their namesake saint. On the secular side, October is Pregnancy and Infant Loss Awareness Month, a time of memorial services, fundraising races/walks, or candle-lighting ceremonies from local support groups to raise awareness and commemorate babies lost to miscarriage, stillbirth, or infant loss.

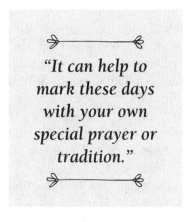

"It can help to mark these days with your own special prayer or tradition."

It can help to mark these days with your own special prayer or tradition. You might visit the cemetery, have a memorial Mass celebrated, or make a donation to a favorite charity or local pregnancy center. Some families celebrate their baby's "birthday into heaven" with a special meal or dessert. Other parents have adopted the habit of doing acts of kindness in their child's honor or writing a letter to them on their anniversary each year.

You may find that the days leading up to significant dates are harder than the actual anniversary. Often the anticipation of an anniversary triggers more grief than the day itself. Be gentle with yourself if this is the case. Try to clear extra space in your work or personal calendar to give yourself time for rest and quiet, to pray and prepare. Ultimately, there is no perfect way to handle difficult anniversaries, so don't feel guilty about how you decide to observe a particular day (or not). Your love for your child is not defined by a date on the calendar. Over time, remembering your baby will become less painful, even if it doesn't feel like it today.

Holidays and feasts

Mother's Day and Father's Day
Holidays celebrating parenthood can be particularly hard after miscarriage, especially if you do not have other living children and the world does not recognize you as a parent. Even attending Mass can be challenging on Mother's Day and Father's Day, when there are special blessings prayed over parents. You may decide to go to the vigil Mass on Saturday instead or to attend Mass at a church or chapel where the emphasis is less likely to be on the secular holiday (such as a convent, monastery, or a Newman Center at a local college). You may still decide to celebrate your spouse in a special way, for example, with a card, gift, or special meal at home.

Making alternative plans for the holiday can help, too. Take a walk, get some exercise, eat good food, or distract yourself with a new project. If your extended family typically gathers on these holidays, you may want to consider making plans to get together on another day if the holiday is simply too painful. Protecting your heart is not a selfish act when you are grieving a significant loss.

Christmas and Easter
The biggest celebrations of the Church year can be difficult days

when you are grieving. Especially when popular traditions are centered around children — like Christmas morning presents and Easter egg hunts — the holidays can be a painful reminder of what you do not have. Praying and preparing in advance can help you navigate difficult situations before they arise. Sit down with your spouse and talk about what you want to do and not do for the holidays. What traditions do you want to continue? What do you want to take a break from this year? Which gatherings or traditions are you looking forward to? Which are you dreading? Give yourself permission to decline invitations or to leave parties early. You don't have to make this year the same as last — or next.

Consider starting your own tradition that includes remembering your child. You might light a special candle at your holiday table in honor of your baby or mention their name in prayer before a special meal. Even if it is a ritual or prayer that you save for the quiet of your own home, you can still bring your child's memory into your celebrations.

Another way to keep your child's memory alive is to make a donation in their honor. For Christmas, you could slip a note into a stocking with the name of the charity you are supporting in their honor. Or you could donate a gift of clothing or toys to match the age and gender of your child. Parishes often offer the option of donating Christmas or Easter flowers in memory of the deceased, so you could include your child in your parish's celebration in this way, too. Talking about a creative, meaningful way to include your baby in the holidays can be a positive, proactive approach.

You may also find that certain aspects of the Church's feasts hold new meaning after suffering the loss of your child. For example, Christ's passion and death on Good Friday remind us that it was "our sufferings he endured … by his wounds we were healed" (Is 53:4–5). Holy Saturday invites us to recall how Jesus' friends were grieving his death, still awaiting the glory about to be revealed to them. Grief can feel like the darkness of Good Friday or the waiting of Holy Saturday. But the paschal mystery at the heart of our faith includes both the dying and the rising of Christ. While the fullness of Easter joy awaits us in eternal life, we can still rejoice in the hope of resurrection for ourselves and our children.

All Saints' Day and All Souls' Day

The solemnities of All Saints' Day (November 1) and All Souls' Day (November 2) offer poignant, prayerful moments to remember your child. All Saints' Day celebrates those who are in heaven (all saints, known and unknown), while All Souls' commemorates all those who have died. Since All Saints' Day is a holy day of obligation, you may wish to take this day to remember your tiny saint, pray for their intercession, and light a candle in their honor. But both feast days speak to our Church's belief in the sanctity of all life and the eternal nature of each human soul. These feasts invite us to thank God for the communion of saints and to pray for the strength of faith to lead us to heaven. If your child was buried, the Feast of All Souls is a fitting time to visit the cemetery or columbarium. Otherwise you can light a votive candle in honor of your baby at church or at home.

Feast of the Holy Innocents

While a tragic massacre may not seem like a day that any bereaved parent would want to remember, the feast of the baby boys in Bethlehem killed by King Herod's command gives us an opportunity to lament the desolation of losing a child. The Gospel for the day (December 28) speaks of the parents' sobbing and weeping at the death of their sons (Mt 2:13–18). Caryll Houselander, a twentieth-century Catholic laywoman and spiritual writer, wrote a striking reflection in *The Passion of the Infant Christ* on the meaning of the Feast of the Holy Innocents for those who mourn the loss of a child: "Baptized in blood, those little children were among the first comers to heaven. Fittingly they, with their tiny King, are the founders of the Kingdom of Children. We celebrate their feast with joy; it is the most lyrical in the year. They reach down their small hands to comfort every father or mother bereaved of a child. They are the first who have proved that the Passion of Christ can be lived in a tiny span by little ones."[13] The Holy Innocents remind grieving parents that the Church weeps with us.

Prayer

Remembering your baby can be as simple as including your child

---

13. Quoted in Thomas Hoffman, ed., *A Child in Winter: Advent, Christmas and Epiphany with Caryll Houselander* (Sheed & Ward: Franklin, WI, 2000), 109-110.

in your daily prayers. You can ask for their intercession and include their name when you pray a Litany of Saints. Prayer always offers an immediate way to connect with your child, to thank God for the gift of your baby in your life, and to ask for grace and mercy in your grief.

Each Mass offers a moving way to remember your baby, since the hope of heaven is woven into the Eucharist: "Finally, by the Eucharistic celebration we already unite ourselves with the heavenly liturgy and anticipate eternal life, when God will be all in all" (CCC 1326). The celebration of the Eucharist is a moment of unity with all the saints in heaven — including, we hope, our beloved babies: "To the offering of Christ are united not only the members still here on earth, but also those already *in the glory of heaven*. In communion with and commemorating the Blessed Virgin Mary and all the saints, the Church offers the Eucharistic sacrifice" (CCC 1370, emphasis original).

The Mass offers several moments that may serve as reminders of your child. The Eucharistic Prayer always includes a prayer for those who have died — for example, "Remember also our brothers and sisters who have fallen asleep in the hope of the resurrection, and all who have died in your mercy: welcome them into the light of your face" (Eucharistic Prayer II). The Nicene Creed also reminds us that God is the Author of Life, the one who gave us our child: "I believe in the Holy Spirit, the Lord, the giver of life." Similarly, at the end of the Creed we profess our belief in eternal life: "I look forward to the resurrection of the dead and the life of the world to come." The idea of looking forward to resurrection resonates with our longing as grieving parents to see our children again one day, keeping our eyes fixed on the hope of heaven.

Prayers on miscarriage

Grief can show up on anticipated anniversaries or surprise us in unexpected moments. Turning to prayer whenever grief arises is the impulse of lament — a traditional form of prayer found throughout Scripture, especially in the psalms. To mark the milestones of the first year of grief, the following prayers drawn from Scripture turn our thoughts back to God throughout the changing emotions and experiences after miscarriage.

FOR THE WEEK AFTER MISCARRIAGE
"Out of the depths I call to you, LORD;
Lord, hear my cry!" (Ps 130:1–2)
* * *

God of mercy, hear our prayer.
From the depths of our grief, answer us.

Our hearts break at the loss of our child.
Our minds struggle to understand.

Just days ago we held the hope of new life.
We carried the joy of a child to raise.

Now death has taken what we love.
Sorrow darkens our days and steals our nights.

We cling to you in our grief, God of hope.
We entrust our baby to your mercy.

Help us to believe we will be with our child again one day.
Help us to trust in the promise of heaven.

In the name of your Son, we pray.
Amen.

FOR ONE MONTH AFTER MISCARRIAGE
"But here I am miserable and in pain;
let your saving help protect me, God." (Ps 69:30)
* * *

Save us, God, from the pit of despair.
Rescue us from the darkness of grief.
As weeks pass and the world moves on,
We are left alone, mourning for our child.

When we feel far from you, draw near to our side.
When we feel overwhelmed by pain, grant us peace.

Lift our eyes to you, Lord.
Help us trust in your healing power.

Hold our child in your love.
Guard his/her memory in our hearts.

In Jesus' name, we pray.
Amen.

FOR SIX MONTHS AFTER MISCARRIAGE

"Blessed are they who mourn,
    for they will be comforted." (Mt 5:4)

* * *

God of comfort,
Six months have passed since our baby died.
Half a year can feel like a lifetime — or like no time at all.

We still dream of our baby,
Imagining what life would be like if our child had lived.
Our hearts ache.

Yet we see the gifts of your comfort, too:
Moments of peace in prayer,
Unexpected growth in wisdom,
Relationships that have deepened, even as others have slipped away.
Our life has known mourning and blessing:
The good you have brought from suffering,
The new life you have raised from death.

Continue to guide, bless, and comfort us,
O God of goodness.
Keep our sight fixed on heaven
And your promise of eternal life,
Where tears will be no more and death will be destroyed,
Where we will rest safe in your embrace,
Together in joy forever.

In the hope of the Holy Spirit, we pray.
Amen.

FOR THE ORIGINAL DUE DATE
"Jesus said to her, 'Woman, why are you weeping? Whom are you looking for?'" (Jn 20:15)
* * *

Lord, today is hard.
Today feels empty.
Today could have been so different.

Today as we remember our child,
As we hold our baby in our hearts
Instead of our arms,
As we mourn in quiet
Instead of wait in joy,
Comfort our sorrow with your love.

Open our eyes to see you here,
To find you in this empty space.
Be with us as we hold vigil
On this hard and heavy day,
Trying not to live in anger or envy
Of what could have been.

Help us to search
Not for a different life than what we have been given,
But for you —
In the midst of the life we have.

Deepen our faith in your promise,
Our hope in your love,
And our trust in your resurrection.
Amen.

FOR A YEAR AFTER MISCARRIAGE
"There is an appointed time for everything,

and a time for every affair under the heavens." (Eccl 3:1)
* * *

Eternal God,
On this hard and holy day,
Remembering the loss of our child,
We cry out to you.

As we mark the day when our lives changed forever,
Help us to see the times of joy and sorrow that this year has brought.

One year ago,
It was a time of death and a time to weep.
Yet in the months since,
There has been time to heal,
Even time to laugh.

This year has brought times we loved, and times we hated,
Time when our hearts raged, and time when we felt peace.
We have known times to embrace, and times to keep from embracing,
Times to be silent, and times to speak.

One year ago,
Our hopes were torn apart.
Yet now you call us to rebuild,
To gather new strength even as we remember.

With all that we have lost,
Still we seek your face.
With all that has been broken,
Still we believe you can create anew.

God of all time, even in today's sorrow,
Lift our hearts to see the dawn of your hope.
Let us praise forever the glory of your name,
As it was in the beginning, is now, and ever shall be.
Amen.

FOR THE YEARLY ANNIVERSARY OF A MISCARRIAGE

"Do not fear, for I have redeemed you;
    I have called you by name: you are mine.
When you pass through waters, I will be with you;
    through rivers, you shall not be swept away." (Is 43:1–2)
***

God of hope, help us to trust in your promises.
Help us to remember your faithfulness:
That if you have brought us this far,
You will continue to carry us all the way.

In the years of missing our baby,
We have walked through the fires of anger,
The rivers of grief,
And the floods of sorrow.
But you have not let them destroy us.

Let us trust in your promises.
Help us not to fear what lies ahead,
For you have made a way through the wilderness of grief.

Help us to listen for your call,
To believe in your love,
And to trust in your way.
Amen.

FOR UNEXPECTED MOMENTS OF GRIEF

"They woke him and said to him, 'Teacher, do you not care that we are perishing?' He woke up, rebuked the wind, and said to the sea, 'Quiet! Be still!'" (Mk 4: 38–39)
***

Jesus, your word quieted the chaos and stilled the storm.
When the night was dark and the waves were high,
You saved your friends from fear.
You rescued them from death.

Calm the grief that rises up within me,

The sorrow that steals my breath and aches my heart.
Let it remind me of my great love for my child,
But let it not send me sinking into despair.

Keep my eyes upon your light.
Deepen my faith,
Draw my heart close to yours.
Grant, I pray, your mercy and rest.

You are the way that leads me home,
The peace my soul seeks,
And the promise of the heavenly shore
Where your beloved saints, great and small,
Will together behold the beauty of your face.

In faith I pray.
Amen.

REFLECTION QUESTIONS

How do you want to prepare for upcoming holidays or anniversaries?

What ideas might you want to try for remembering your baby?

Kellie and Jason's story

I am the mother of three precious souls: one here on earth and two in heaven. I know two different sides of loss, one where you can prepare (as much as possible anyway), after an adverse prenatal diagnosis. You have memories and mementos of your child that can carry you through the toughest moments of grief. That's my Lily. Losing her shattered my world, but I have a trunk full of her things and photos on the wall that I can wrap myself in when the waves of grief crash into me.

The other side of loss is the one you didn't see coming at all. It knocks you over like a freight train and leaves you gasping for breath. There's nothing to console you if you only have an ultrasound picture or possibly a few cards of sympathy. That's my littlest Clare. Losing her rocked me in ways I never imagined.

Everything about her story was perfect. She was supposed to be my rainbow baby, my redemption story after a tremendous year of grief after losing Lily. God told me I was pregnant with Clare before a pregnancy test ever could. Even though my mind was so worried that she could have the same defect as Lily, my heart was at peace because she seemed meant to be. I vividly heard God say, "I have a child for you."

But then the ultrasound showed no heartbeat at eight weeks. I had been worrying and praying so much for a round head, that the lack of a heartbeat was nowhere near my radar. But I knew before they even told me. I knew how a flickering heart should look, and I knew hers was not flickering. I couldn't even look at my husband because I already knew the hurt in his eyes. My mind immediately went back to that fateful day when they told us Lily was "incompatible with life." That day is when I truly learned about despair, the absence of hope.

The rest of that year was isolating and lonely. I was no longer pregnant, but my mind couldn't escape where I knew my pregnancy should be. Each week or month that I passed a pregnancy milestone was like a new dagger in my empty womb.

Being pregnant with Lily and knowing we would lose her was hard, but we pressed on because we knew meeting her would help us to bear the weight of grief. In the weeks and months following her diagnosis, the despair was replaced with the anticipated joy of finally getting to meet her. We could gather symbolic gifts for her, special outfits and blankets, pictures of my pregnancy, and so much more. I miss her terribly every single day, but I can look at her photos on the wall or the molds of her hands and feet and find comfort and peace. Because she was here, she is real, and she is mine.

Clare was here, too. She is real, and she is mine also. But no one could see that. It doesn't mean I miss her less. Some days the pain of missing Clare is magnified because of all the things I don't have: pictures, outfits, or any memory of holding her that I can cling to. The despair wasn't replaced with the joy of meeting her. We didn't have the chance to memorize all her sweet details. I only have one tiny box with a handful of cards and one ultrasound picture.

Some will say this is a blessing. Because you can't miss what you never had, right? Yet I do. I grieve every moment I am missing with both of my daughters. I love them both and miss them each tremendously. Lily and Clare are both buried in the same cemetery, not far from one another. It gives me some peace when I think of them together. We visit often, now bringing two sets of decorations to honor our girls. We pray family rosaries and end each decade with, "Lily and Clare, pray for us." Our four-year-old son sees a spectacular sunset and says, "It's a kiss from Lily and Clare."

At least a hundred times a day, I imagine everything that should be, exactly where they would fit in our lives. I see Lily toddling right behind her brother and Clare trying to keep up with them both. Yet every single day I still manage to find hope in what is, in this reality of life amid loss where we find ourselves, between here and there. Every single day, I beg and plead with God for all that seems impossible. I ask for faith that surpasses my understanding and can hope against hope. I pray over and over, "Teach me Lord to pray with my whole heart, 'Jesus, I trust in You.'"

Your relationship with each other

To understand the impact of miscarriage on a marriage, picture your relationship placed in the intense pressure and heat of a forge. As time passes, you will emerge from the furnace. But the question is whether your marriage will come out stronger, whether it will crack in painful ways, or whether it could fall apart.

Couples may worry about the long-term impact of grief on their marriage. You may have heard that couples who lose a child are more likely to divorce. While stress is normal after such a significant loss, this does not have to threaten the commitment of your marriage. Indeed, the opposite can be true: understanding potential challenges to your marriage can encourage and empower you to focus more love and attention on your relationship.

When you professed your wedding vows to each other, you promised to be faithful in good times and in bad, in sickness and in health, to love and honor each other all the days of your life. If you were married in the Catholic Church, you agreed to accept children lovingly from God. While this promise has likely brought more sorrow than you ever expected, your commitment to each other can still stand firm in the face of the suffering you have endured. The truth is that being married is easy when things are better, richer, and healthy. Naturally most newlyweds prefer to picture only good times ahead. When life turns worse, poorer, and sicker, we have to turn to God and each other for the strength to keep going.

There is no quick "fix" for the loss of a baby. When a couple is busy, especially if they have other children, it can be difficult to sit down and have a conversation about how to mourn and heal together. You may need to invest energy and time in learning new ways to communicate after loss. Whenever people try something different — a new recipe, a new sport, or a trip to a new city — they often seek the advice of someone who already knows what it is like. Going through the jarring experience of miscarriage (even if it isn't your first loss) may mean you need to seek out the counsel of a trusted priest, therapist, or friend who can offer objective and sound advice. Drawing together the support of those who want to help you stay committed to your spouse can give you strength and hope.

As a couple, we found it easier to talk and pray together about grief at the end of the day. The quiet moments before going to sleep can be some of the most sacred and vulnerable moments in married life. Even when we struggled to find the words to pray together, we could pray an Our Father to remind us of our shared trust in God. We also found comfort in the liturgy and sacraments of the Church. Going to Mass together was particularly important to us in grief. Often one of us would find a word in Scripture, a message from the homily, or a line from a hymn that spoke to where we were in our grief. This became the catalyst for conversations after Mass that we might not have normally had otherwise.

Ways to strengthen your marriage

Miscarriage is likely one of the hardest things you have been through, both as individuals and as a couple. Be gentle with each other. Grief sometimes gets worse before it gets better. Some couples say that four to six months after their loss can feel even harder than the initial days, once the reality of grief sets in. You may find that this later point is when you need more support as a couple — from each other or from others who have had similar losses. Remember that if you decide to seek counseling or a support group, you may have to try several before finding a good fit.

As a couple, we received important help from our experience with counseling after the death of our twins. We found a couple's therapist who specialized in grief and child loss, and her guidance and wisdom helped us to sort through our emotions and experiences in healthy ways. We also attended a support group for pregnancy and infant loss at our local hospital (and later joined the companion group for pregnancy after loss). Sitting around the table with other couples who understood our pain was an important source of empathy and solidarity that we could not find anywhere else. We

"Be gentle with each other. Grief sometimes gets worse before it gets better."

shared ways to cope with work, family, and friends after grief; we learned how to prepare in advance for difficult days like holidays and anniversaries; we even laughed together at experiences surrounding grief that no one else in our life could understand. We often went out for dinner together after the support group meetings so that we could have private time together to talk. These meals stand among our most important times of connection during the hardest months of grief.

We also brought our children to a family retreat at Faith's Lodge, a nationally renowned retreat center that offers programming for bereaved parents and grieving families. The chance to meet other families with similar losses and to spend peaceful time with our living children remembering and giving thanks for the lives of our babies was a beautiful opportunity for our family — and an important healing time for our kids as well.

Closer to home, Franco made a garden in our yard in honor of our babies, and we continue to tend this ground as a sacred place of connection to them. Each Mother's Day and Father's Day, we remember the children we have lost by including their names on a card and in our prayers. Even though we have living children, these holidays remain complicated for both of us as bereaved parents. So we always try to find a small way to incorporate all our children.

Strengthening your marriage after loss can start in the simplest ways:

- Set a reminder in your calendar for difficult dates (e.g., the day you learned you were expecting, the anniversary of the miscarriage, or the original due date)
- Spend quality time together — a date night, a weekend away, or a walk outside
- Go to Mass together
- Send an email or text during the day to let your spouse know you're thinking of them
- Pray together at night before bed or in the morning before work
- Surprise your spouse by doing some of their household tasks for them
- Practice patience and forgiveness with each other

- Make your marriage a priority: in prayer, in thought, in daily action, and in service

Intimacy after loss is another area of your relationship that requires loving attention and communication, perhaps more now than ever before. Even if you are physically ready to resume sex again, grief can complicate what might have been an easy and enjoyable part of your marriage before miscarriage. The vulnerability of connecting with your spouse, as well as any lingering physical issues after healing from your loss, can make intimacy a daunting prospect for even the most loving couples. What's more, the woman's cycles may not return to normal right after miscarriage, which can be challenging and frustrating whether or not you are hoping to conceive again. If you are using natural family planning after miscarriage, be sure to consult your instructor for how to chart and monitor these changes in your cycle accurately.

The wisdom of Ecclesiastes speaks to the changing rhythms throughout the length of a marriage, a comforting reminder that the state of sexuality in your marriage right now will not remain the same forever. In every life, there is "a time to embrace and a time to be far from embraces" (Eccl 3:5). Communicating about your needs and desires, being patient with your spouse, and demonstrating your love in other tangible ways can help strengthen your marriage as you move through these times of change together.

Your relationship with God

Relationships in your life have changed because of your miscarriage. Maybe a family member was not able to support you in your grief, and your relationship is now strained. Maybe an acquaintance shared their own story of loss, and you forged a strong new connection. Your relationship with God is no different: it may have changed in big or small ways because of your loss.

Paying attention to the relationship between you and God is just as important as paying attention to the relationship between you and your spouse. Though God has not changed, you have. Perhaps you have cast aside notions of God that were untrue. Or perhaps you have discovered a new side of God's love and compassion. You may find yourself filled with questions for God, or you may feel numb and uncertain about what you believe. All your struggles and concerns can be brought to God in prayer.

Returning to Scripture and the sacraments can keep your faith grounded through grief. (See chapters 9 and 10 for prayers to support your faith through grief.) For us, our parish was a huge source of support in grief. After our miscarriage, Laura had a powerful experience after Mass in which a group of parishioners prayed for God's healing to surround her. Their care and concern affirmed how the Church is a community where every life, no matter how brief, is valued and loved. After our twins died, our parish reached out with prayers, helped us to plan their funeral, and continues to pray for them each November as part of our communal prayer for the dead. Their witness to us has been an impetus in our own calling to help other grieving couples. We have also attended a local Mass of God's Children in our archdiocese each October — another example of the Church's compassion for grieving parents. (See Appendix B for a list of ways that local parishes can reach out after the loss of a child and Appendix C for sample prayers for a Mass of God's Children.)

There is no single outcome of suffering and tragedy on a grieving parent's faith. Prayer keeps some parents going after loss; for others, prayer feels nearly impossible, especially if they prayed for God to save their baby and their prayer was not answered as they hoped. Some cling to God and find their faith deepen in unexpected ways. Others are surprised by their anger, depression, doubt, or resentment.

Death can bring us face to face with what has previously been a theoretical understanding of our faith. We know that God lets bad things happen, but when it happens to us and our child, the acuteness of the loss changes everything. A personal and painful encounter with death asks us to reflect on how suffering has impacted our faith. What does this experience mean for our relationship with God, as well as God's role in our marriage?

People often compare the time after loss to being in the wilderness, feeling abandoned and searching for God, or wandering in the desert. Scripture is full of these "desert stories" but also reminds us that the wilderness is never where God asks us to stay. The Israelites were led through the desert into a new home. Jesus left the desert after forty days to begin his new ministry. Wilderness is a journey, not an end in itself. No matter how desolate we may feel, we can still trust that God is leading us somewhere.

Changes over time

After miscarriage, you are changed. So is your husband or wife. This loss will impact your relationship, but your commitment to each other does not have to weaken. It is common to have times when the bond between you is strong and times when you feel distant from each other. Some couples feel closer than ever immediately after miscarriage, but then feel like they are drifting apart in the weeks and months that follow. Others feel isolated at the beginning and then gradually make their way back to each other as time passes. Ebbs and flows are natural in any relationship, although they can feel amplified because of the intensity of grief.

The Swiss psychiatrist Elisabeth Kübler-Ross proposed a now-famous model of 5 stages of grief: denial, anger, bargaining, depression, and acceptance. While these stages are not a linear progression, they describe shifts in grief over time that many people experience. Such changes can be challenging, requiring patience and the reminder that both partners in the marriage are trying to figure out their world after miscarriage.

While each couple's experience is unique, we found it helpful to hear how others had experienced changes (and even growth) in grief — especially in the early months when it felt impossible to imagine that we would ever experience joy or happiness again. During one low point, Franco walked into the office of a coworker who had gone through a similar loss and asked, "Will life ever get better?" The first year was intensely difficult: getting through each holiday and anniversary, imagining how our baby would have been growing each month, and trying to come to terms with what we had suffered.

The second year brought different shades of hard. Support from family and friends was not as immediate as in earlier months, because people had naturally turned back to their own lives and concerns. Yet we had to settle into the reality that this was our life and grief would not disappear just because we had survived the first year.

The third year finally turned a corner in a place of greater peace and stability. We could feel God as present with us in our healing as in our grief. We came to see how our love for our child would never fade, but our grief was becoming more manageable: a reality that we could carry with us, rather than an overwhelming darkness.

The beauty of remaining committed in marriage is the strength that comes from enduring trials together. There is comfort in knowing that, though grief may be bewildering, challenging, and foreign, the person you love most remains with you through it. The trials you endure together can eventually bring you closer together. When our marriage vows move from words spoken to actions taken, it deepens the love that we share and our faith in God at work in our vocation.

As the opening Scripture verse from this chapter reminds us, any present suffering is never the end of the story God is writing as the author of our lives. God is always working to bring good out of pain and sorrow. Suffering and loss can ultimately bear unexpected fruits for your marriage: closer intimacy, deeper trust, better communication, or greater compassion. While we never could have imagined that miscarriage and loss would have brought any goodness to our lives, we can see now that God has given powerful graces for our marriage through grief: greater compassion for those who suffer, sharper clarity in our own callings, deeper generosity to those in need, a stronger desire to be of service to others, and a clearer priority of our faith and family over anything else in our lives.

As you continue to work through your grief together, do not lose sight of the small (or big) graces that God has brought to your relationship in life after loss. The paschal mystery — Christ's dying and rising to new life — is also the shape of each Christian's life, when we trust that God can bring life from death. Like seeds in winter, some new creation may be waiting to spring forth when we least expect it.

REFLECTION QUESTIONS

How has your miscarriage affected your marriage?

What do you hope for your marriage a year from now? Ten years from now?

Mike and Kateri's story

Our journey of loss has intermingled moments of suffering with moments of celebration. We found out we were losing our first baby just days after we celebrated our first anniversary; Kateri labored and lost the baby nearly a week later, during a graduation party. Our second miscarriage was discovered at a doctor's appointment on the day of a sister's graduation party; this little love would have had a Christmastime birthday just like the first baby we lost.

Our third loss was an early miscarriage, whom we lost just two days after Kateri announced the pregnancy to Mike as his Valentine's Day gift; that baby was due on Kateri's birthday. Our fourth miscarriage was first suspected on the day of a family graduation party; this would-have-been-New Year's baby was delivered several weeks later, in the middle of our daughter's birthday party. So the line between our experience of suffering and celebration is so fine that we can hardly distinguish where one ends and the other begins.

It has been over nine years since we lost our first baby. We were then blessed with three healthy, happy children who bring joyous chaos into our home each day, before losing three more babies. But even our pregnancies that brought living children were marked by the tension between good and difficult after first knowing the all-too-real hurt of miscarriage.

Despite being excited and overjoyed about each new life, our pregnancies have also carried extreme fear and anxiety. Every decision to try again has been a process mixed with this same tension of hope and fear. Even sex itself becomes more complicated. The ever-present realization that sex means being open not only to possible life, but also the great potential for loss again, adds sorrow to the beauty. The entanglement of struggle and blessing is a reality in so many aspects of our relationship.

Not a day has gone by that we do not think of the babies we've lost. Speaking about it, however, has been a different story. For Mike, emotions have never been overtly expressed, and grief — especially the grief of miscarriage — has been no exception. Dealing with it inwardly, coupled with the challenge of not knowing what to say to support Kateri (and the fear of breaking down if he tried to talk about it), led to considerable silence.

Kateri is an outwardly emotional person. When she longed to talk about miscarriage, Mike's silence felt as though he were ignoring that their child had existed. This added to the penetrating sense of loneliness that already accompanied her grief, leaving her to turn inward and feel silenced as well. The different ways in which we dealt with grief have been the most challenging part of our loss and of our marriage.

Yet over time we have also seen such good come from our losses. Despite the intense struggle throughout and after our miscarriages, we have come to understand better how each of us deals with grief. What started out as anger and resentment at our differences grew into greater respect and greater love. So while we cannot say that we handled it "together," we can say that we have grown because of it. Good and bad, joy and sorrow, suffering and celebration are woven together — not only in our relationship to one another, but also in our relationships to God and to the Church.

Losing our first baby was crushing to Mike's relationship with God, which was already in a rough place. It took years, and having our other children, to rebuild this relationship. But our subsequent miscarriages were a new kind of crushing loss. Not only did we lose our children, but we also lost the dream of having the big family we wanted our kids to have. Knowing the grace of having children made it much harder to lose them.

Kateri's anger grew as well. Hers was at the Church. As a lay minister who had always been close to the Church, she suddenly found herself furious at what she perceived to be a disconnect between the abundant resources invested in protecting early life as a pro-life Church and what felt like a lack of resources for those struggling with this kind of early loss. She felt ignored in her grief each time. It wasn't until a powerful experience of the Sacrament of Reconciliation years later that she finally found the courage and "permission" she needed to ask for support.

After our fourth miscarriage, Kateri reached out more intentionally, and our faith community was very compassionate. Our relationship to the parish community, and the God they represent, has grown stronger as a result of our difficult journey.

There is much we continue to suffer from, and yet much we have to celebrate. Celebrations have been central in the memories we have of our short time with our babies. So despite all the struggle that continues to accompany their absence in our lives, we choose to celebrate. We eat a special treat on their birthdays (due dates) each year. We buy a gift for their would-have-been age and gender to donate each Christmas. We include them in our family's prayers of thanksgiving each night.

The fact that our suffering of miscarriage always took place in a context of celebration does not seem coincidental to us. While a painful intermingling at first, we have come to see that perhaps God has placed these two so close together on the calendar to remind us that he does not wish us to linger in suffering. It is a long journey, as grief does not follow a timeline. There has been great sorrow, fear, and pain. Yet we have seen blessing, hope, and joy. The beautiful and the difficult have become so intertwined that we can hardly differentiate any more. This is the reality of loss. But more than that, this is family; this is marriage; this is life. This is our story.

Chapter 12

What Comes Next

Remembering it over and over,
my soul is downcast.
But this I will call to mind;
therefore I will hope:
The Lord's acts of mercy are not exhausted,
his compassion is not spent;
They are renewed each morning —
great is your faithfulness!
The Lord is my portion, I tell myself,
therefore I will hope in him.
The Lord is good to those who trust in him,
to the one that seeks him;
It is good to hope in silence
for the Lord's deliverance. (Lam 3:20–26)

What will the future hold? There is no harder evidence of life's uncertainty than the loss of a child. As grieving parents, we have learned that we must live with loss, carrying the love of our children into our lives moving forward. While the shift from surviving to thriving can take a long time, the work of grief asks us to integrate loss into our lives, not to forget it or suppress it. As you begin a new chapter, the depth of your loss does not lessen — but you grow stronger. Grief is no longer a world you live in, but a reality you live with as part of the memory and legacy of your child.

Our faith teaches us that life begins at conception, and so does our journey as parents. Implicit in this truth is the understanding that once you are a parent, you never stop being a parent. Your child is your child forever, regardless of how long they were alive in this world. This is a perspective that can be difficult to understand — especially for those who do not have living children — but it is a fact. The pain that persists over the years is a testament to the truth that you are still a parent to your child who died. No matter what comes next, your child has changed you forever.

Pregnancy after loss

The majority of parents who try to conceive again after miscarriage go on to have a healthy pregnancy. You should consult your doctor about your specific situation, but generally couples are able to start trying to conceive shortly after miscarriage. Yet physical health is not the only consideration. Discerning whether you are emotionally and spiritually ready for pregnancy after loss is a big question — now that you know being open to life means being open to loss.

Pregnancy after loss raises many questions for parents:

- Can I be excited about this new baby?
- What if this baby dies, too?
- Can I trust God?
- Will I love this baby more than the baby we lost?
- Will other people forget about our miscarriage?
- What will parenting this baby be like?

Spouses navigate the challenges and fears of pregnancy after loss differently. Excitement may seem to replace grief for one parent, while the complexity of grieving for one child while preparing to welcome a new baby can feel overwhelming for the other. Communication and compassion are the best tools to support each other in your marriage through pregnancy after loss. You may also wish to ask your priest or deacon to bless your baby with the Rite of Blessing of a Child in the Womb or to pray the Order for the Blessing of Parents before Childbirth (both found online at usccb.org).

This pregnancy will likely be harder than any earlier pregnancies. You may not feel as excited or hopeful, which is natural after what you have experienced. Pregnancy after loss brings a roller coaster of emotions. The blissful innocence of preparing to welcome a baby has disappeared. Instead, you cautiously guard your heart and worry about what could go wrong.

Anxiety during pregnancy after loss is natural and common. Milestone markers — like reaching the week when you miscarried or preparing for routine ultrasounds — can be triggers for grief. Returning to the same hospital or doctor's office can be intensely emotional, especially when preparing for birth. Be sure your doctor or midwife can understand and accommodate your increased concerns about this new pregnancy, given what you have been through in the past. If you are having intense anxiety, panic attacks, or suicidal thoughts, contact a health care professional immediately to get help.

Pregnancy after loss is not just a physical experience, but a spiritual journey as well. It can be intense and isolating, as it raises hard questions about life, death, and God — just like grief. Understanding the spiritual challenges of pregnancy after miscarriage, holding fast to God's Word, and turning to prayer can lead to hope through fear and make pregnancy less daunting. Here are four truths about pregnancy after loss and the ways they invite us to grow in faith:

1. Pregnancy after loss means there are no guarantees. Spiritually, the invitation is to trust.

The loss of a baby disrupts the natural order: you expected that your children would outlive you. After miscarriage, you no longer assume anything about how your life or this new child's life will turn out. You might be angry or feel like God has betrayed you. You may struggle to believe that this journey will end well.

But trust is not a one-time decision. With God's love and guidance, you can learn to believe in life's possibilities in new ways. Even when you cannot predict for certain what will happen next, the Lord's faithful companionship remains. God has been with you in the past, God is here in the present, and God will be with you in the future.

> "It is the LORD who goes before you; he will be with you and will never fail you or forsake you. So do not fear or be dismayed." (Dt 31:8)

2. Pregnancy after loss brings a daily temptation to despair. Spiritually, the invitation is to hope.

When you know the worst that can happen, it is hard to stop thinking it could happen again. You may delay sharing the news that you're expecting, because you fear turning around to share sad news again.

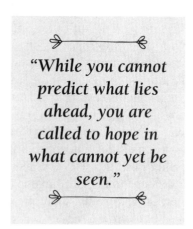

"While you cannot predict what lies ahead, you are called to hope in what cannot yet be seen."

You might hold off preparing for the baby because you do not want to take apart another nursery. You can feel like you are holding your breath, waiting for the other shoe to drop. Despair thrives under these conditions.

While you cannot predict what lies ahead, you are called to hope in what cannot yet be seen. This is the fundamental stance of Christians toward the world, believing in the resurrection. Hope is a gift given to each of us by God and a virtue that can be deepened with practice. Choosing hope over despair each day is a radical act of faith. The strength of Scripture and the saints can lead us to grow in hope as people of the resurrection.

> "For in hope we were saved. Now hope that sees for itself is not hope. For who hopes for what one sees? But if we hope for

what we do not see, we wait with endurance." (Rom 8:24–25)

3. Pregnancy after loss can lead to anger and jealousy. Spiritually, the invitation is to seek peace.

Even after you are expecting again, you may still envy other parents. It is tempting to stew in anger and jealousy, wondering why loss had to happen to you. You might feel flooded with negativity and worry how your emotions are affecting your baby. You may keep asking why God let this suffering happen.

In the stage of life when peers are having babies, you often find yourself in conversations about pregnancy and parenting. You can pray for God's grace to grow in compassion for others as you learn how to navigate these emotional triggers. You can also practice compassion toward yourself and excuse yourself from difficult situations to protect your heart. Just as God shows great mercy toward you, so can you find peace in choosing mercy over jealousy.

> "Have no anxiety at all, but in everything, by prayer and petition, with thanksgiving, make your requests known to God. Then the peace of God that surpasses all understanding will guard your hearts and minds in Christ Jesus." (Phil 4:6–7)

4. Pregnancy after loss knows you cannot control. Spiritually, the invitation is to practice humility.

Today's parenting culture can lead you to believe everything is up to you: if you make all the best decisions, your child will "turn out right." But you know the opposite is true: you could not control what happened with your last pregnancy. While this feels frightening, it is also the beginning of humility. Because we cannot control so much about our lives, we can only rely on God. Remembering how you and your child are held within a wider embrace of God's love can start to free you from anxiety and the desire to control.

Whenever you start to worry about "what if," you can remember that you have the choice of where to dwell in your thoughts. Do you want to live in a dark, unknown future that has not yet happened? Or do you want to live in the possibility of goodness? Humility gently reorients your thoughts, reminding you that your life and your baby's life are held in the hands of God.

> "Can any of you by worrying add a single moment to your life-span?... But seek first for the kingdom [of God] and his righteousness, and all these things will be given you besides." (Mt 6:27, 33)

Parenting after loss

In recent years the phrase "rainbow baby" has become a popular term to describe a child born after loss as a rainbow after the storm. Some parents find this to be a beautiful metaphor, while others resist comparing the death of their baby to a storm. No matter how you choose to see your new baby, he or she will bring unexpected joys and challenges to your life. Your parenting — like every other aspect of your life — will be shaped by what came before.

Parenting after loss can be shadowed by anxiety. After losing a baby, you are naturally afraid of what might happen to your child in the future. There is no protection from this pain, no quick fix to free you from fear. But an awareness of your own limits is an invitation to let God's love help you do what you fear you cannot do. No child will ever replace the baby you lost. But you can care for your new baby with new love — a powerful testimony to the strength of your heart as a parent.

Some parents find that grief reemerges in unexpected ways after birth, as their new baby reminds them of what they lost, even while they feel grateful to bring a child home to raise. Take care to monitor your mental health during pregnancy and after birth, since studies have found that both mothers and fathers can experience symptoms of postpartum depression, especially after a previous loss.

Parents often wonder how to tell subsequent children about the sibling that came before them. There is no perfect age or moment to have this conversation, but many families choose to start sharing the story while children are still young, to make their older sibling a normal and natural part of the family. Celebrating that baby's birthday with a special dessert, praying for them by name, and asking them to pray for you are all simple ways to share the baby who came before. Your miscarriage is not a shameful secret to hide away, but part of your family's love and life together that can be shared with your children whenever and however you feel comfortable as parents.

Life after loss

Couples who do not go on to conceive another biological child face unique struggles after miscarriage. If they decide to pursue adoption or foster parenting, they carry grief alongside parenting in particular ways — for example, mourning the biological experiences of pregnancy, birth, or nursing while still celebrating the gift of their child. If a couple already had living children prior to their miscarriage but then does not conceive again, they face the prospect of ending their childbearing years with a loss, not the happy ending of another baby. If a couple remains without living children, they carry the heavy suffering of being parents that the world cannot see or affirm. Each of these experiences brings its own challenges for life after miscarriage.

If you decide to pursue adoption or foster parenting (Claire and Jerry's story)

"But this baby is really yours." "This baby comes from you and Jerry." These were responses when I shared the paradox of my joy over discovering we were pregnant (my second pregnancy, after one early miscarriage and over three years of trying) and my disappointment about having to table our adoption application. It was early in the pregnancy, before I knew that I was carrying identical twins in a high-risk pregnancy. But part of me knew that my chances of a live birth were slim, that we would likely build our family through adoption, and that even in my inner circle, there would be people who considered me less of a mother and consider my adopted child as second-best.

Grief, like joy, can't be quantified. But my husband and I were equally devastated when the ultrasound at thirteen weeks gestation showed ten-week size fetuses without heartbeats. The stark contrast to four weeks earlier — when the babies were moving and their hearts beating — was excruciating. From there, our grief diverged. My husband was ready to resume the adoption process right away, but I needed more time. Less than five months later, when the social worker placed our tiny five-pound baby in our arms, my husband fell in love with him instantly, while it took me a few days. After ten years, I still grieve for my miscarried babies and for the loss of experiences like full-term pregnancy and breastfeeding, while paradoxically rejoicing that my dream of adoption has miraculously been fulfilled.

Occasionally, I still receive comments hinting that my adopted child is something of a consolation prize. Unlike me, my husband is able to let those comments roll off his back. In turn he gets my perspective back on track by reminding me that misguided perceptions don't negate the parental bond we have with our son, which couldn't be stronger if he had been born to us and carried our DNA. Ultimately our different grieving styles have complemented each other and have been a blessing to our marriage and our family.

If the child you lost is your last child
(Eileen and Patrick's story)
On the first day of Advent, I learned I was pregnant. Because my husband Patrick and I are approaching our mid-forties, we were both surprised and excited by the news. We have five young children at home, and I soon began imagining what life would be like with a sixth in our busy, joyful house. But about three weeks after learning of the existence of our new baby, I began bleeding. On Christmas Day, I miscarried.

Losing a baby was not a new experience for us. I miscarried my third pregnancy, and not long after that, we lost twin daughters in stillbirth and infant death to twin-to-twin transfusion syndrome. But losing our last baby hurt my heart in a unique way. It felt like I'd failed my final experience of pregnancy and went out on a sour note.

Because of our age, there is not likely to be another baby to help to redeem the disappointment of that loss. However, we believe that our sadness and suffering is redemptive by itself, if we offer it up and trust God to use it for our good and for his glory. Our losses have given us an eternal perspective, and we look forward to reuniting one day with all of our children in heaven.

If you remain parents without living children
(Mary and Jaime's story)
My husband and I have encountered many anxieties on this heart-breaking journey. After three pregnancies and no births, I often won-

der about my own self-worth. I feel stuck in a limbo of numerous specialist appointments with doctors who are booked for months, just to be passed to another doctor. We see others' dreams coming true around us almost daily.

It is terrible, yet we know that the only way forward is in Christ: "Lord, to whom shall we go?" I think about what an alternative life in not living the Faith would look like, and it would make everything infinitely harder to bear. We have to remain in the Lord. And there are beautiful, wonderful, amazing things happening in our lives that are complete blessings from God. I don't want to lose sight of the forest for the trees.

But it is still heart-wrenching for both of us to see little kids at church or when we are out running errands. It could have been us. It should be us, and yet it may never be us. To come to terms with this — I am not sure we really have. All we can do is hold on to our faith. I know the Lord will see us through, even if the answer isn't what we want. But we have our moments of darkness and despair. Most of the time, we are able to hold on to hope.

The loss of our babies also makes us worry about the general direction of our society. We want to have babies and raise them for the glory of God. Many people are not interested in their children's formation in faith. We just want to know that there will be enough people in future generations to preach Christ to the world.

Growth after loss

Post-traumatic stress is possible after miscarriage (see chapter 4). But researchers are also discovering the reality of "post-traumatic growth" — what happens when tragedy deepens our appreciation of our own strength, our relationships, and the meaning of life. This psychological phenomenon describes what the Christian tradition has long understood: that God can work through the worst to bring life out of death and growth out of loss. Eventually grief will not be the defining darkness hanging over your days, but over time it can lead to deeper faith, trust, or compassion.

Not every couple goes on to conceive, birth, or raise a biological child after miscarriage. Not all couples who hope to foster or adopt are able to bring a child home. But God is at work in every one of our lives, no matter the situation or circumstances. God's plans for us are still good. What lies ahead of us may be possibilities we could never have imagined before miscarriage entered our lives.

Your baby's memory can change your future. It might be as simple as remembering to ask a coworker how he is doing after he and his wife lose a baby. It might be as big as starting an outreach in your parish to help others who have gone through miscarriage. Parents often describe the gift of finding new purpose after loss, sharing their story with someone else in need, or creating community to support others through their grief. When friends, family, or strangers experience suffering, you may be able to reach out with more understanding, love, and compassion because of what you have lived through.

We are different people because our babies existed. We will never forget them. We will never stop missing them or wondering how life might have been different if they had lived. But we can also believe that God will lead us from sorrow to joy and from death to new life. This is the legacy of our children's lives that we will carry with us forever.

> Gracious is the Lord and righteous;
> yes, our God is merciful.
> The Lord protects the simple;
> I was helpless, but he saved me.
> Return, my soul, to your rest;
> the Lord has been very good to you.
> For my soul has been freed from death,
> my eyes from tears, my feet from stumbling.
> I shall walk before the Lord
> in the land of the living. (Ps 116:5–9)

REFLECTION QUESTIONS

What have you learned about yourself, your spouse, or God through miscarriage?

What would you want to say to other parents who have lost a baby?

Jenna and Mike's story

The nurse came into the room and gave me a hug. She said, "I'm so sorry, honey. I'm so, so sorry. You can have more. I know you can. Eventually, you can have more. You don't have to wait; you can have more."

"I don't want more," I thought to myself. "I wanted this one and only this one. Not a different baby, not more babies. This one." I want this one to know me more than just my womb she lived in for nine weeks. I wanted him or her to know more. To nuzzle me in the middle of the night when only my smell and my touch mean everything. To cry for me in her own unique voice. To give life to me as much as we gave life to her.

I didn't want another one. I wanted this one. I want her. I want him. Tears stung my eyes. My breath was gone, and I had no other words. My husband sat next to me, holding my hand. He asked me, off in the distance, "How do you feel?"

I responded, "I feel nothing. I don't have a word for this." It wasn't grief. It wasn't sadness. It was just emptiness with nothingness sprinkled on top. The golden recipe for loss.

I stared off and realized that the nothingness surrounded me. There was nothing I could do to stop it. I was only a victim to its presence. The nothingness weighed heavily in my room, suffocating me until it was hard to breathe. The nothingness sat on my chest and forced me to think about it. Forced me to remember my womb would soon hold nothing.

We went to the midwife's office and had another ultrasound done. It was the same story we had heard days prior: "You are ten weeks, but the baby stopped growing at eight. There is no heartbeat."

"Fetal demise." The most awful words I could have heard.

I had a womb with a child who was lifeless. A child longed for, a child we dreamed for, a child we hoped would be, a child we planned to love. There was no heartbeat.

"So what happens now?" I asked the midwife, who was sitting there with kindness and sorrow in her eyes. She gave me my options. My husband and I chose to pass the baby at home on a day when my mom could take our daughters so just my husband and I could go through this horrible, awful experience alone. Saturday was planned for, and Saturday finally came.

I had asked my fellow sisters in Christ who had miscarried before, "What will this experience be like?" They warned me, those sweet friends of mine. But nothing prepares you for the day you pass your baby. The pain, the trauma, the emotions, the emptiness. Nothing gets you ready for the moment you no longer are holding another human closer than physically possible.

My baby is gone, I thought. My baby is gone. Because what else is there to think?

I grieved differently than Michael, my husband. He told me that he didn't feel the same attachment to the baby that I did. I was in a dark place, and he tried to look after the rest of our family to let me grieve. He tried to move on to give me space to feel.

Eventually he gently held me and whispered, "We've got to keep moving, Jenna. We have three other girls to take care of and to be here for." We definitely drew closer as a couple from this shared experience. I am so grateful I had him.

We are currently pregnant with our fifth pregnancy, and I am so excited, albeit still scared of this baby dying as well. I have been terrified every appointment and ultrasound. Terrified of seeing no heartbeat and hearing those words again: "fetal demise" or "there is no heartbeat." Thankfully, we still have a healthy baby. I am so grateful for the opportunity to have another child.

As a family, we often talk about Brooke (what we named our fourth baby). She is included in our family prayers. One of our daughters talks about her all the time: "I wonder what Brooke is doing in heaven?"

Our daughters' genuine love and openness to Brooke's short life has been a great catalyst to my love and acceptance of our baby. If it weren't for them talking about her, asking about her, and praying for her, I would feel more alone, empty, and isolated. But my daughters allow me to love her. They allow my heart to stay open and not be hardened by miscarriage and loss. We will have a celebration of Brooke's life soon, since the girls keep asking about it. I am so glad I have these girls who teach me what it is to truly love.

Appendix A

Practical Resources

Catholic Miscarriage Support (catholicmiscarriagesupport.com) provides detailed descriptions of the physical process of miscarriage, options for medical management that are in line with Church teaching, and instructions on how to collect and care for the remains of your baby.

Elizabeth Ministry International (elizabethministry.com) offers local chapters and online resources to support women through issues related to childbearing, sexuality, and relationships.

Heaven's Gain (heavensgain.com) provides services and products (including miscarriage kits, urns, and caskets sized for babies in each trimester) for families suffering the loss of a child through miscarriage, stillbirth, or infant death.

Mothering Spirit (motheringspirit.com) offers prayers for miscarriage, suggestions for helping children grieve the loss of a sibling, and practical ideas for family and friends who want to help after a loved one loses a baby.

National Catholic Bioethics Center (ncbcenter.org) includes resources on ethical treatments for pregnancy complications such as ectopic pregnancy.

The Shrine of the Unborn (shrineofholyinnocents.org) at the Church of the Holy Innocents invites parents to enroll in their Book of Life the names of children who have died before or at birth and print a Certificate of Life with their name.

Trappist Caskets (trappistcaskets.com) made by the monks at New Melleray Abbey in Iowa are offered in compassion at no cost to families who have lost a child.

United States Conference of Catholic Bishops (usccb.org) provides the full text of the Blessing of Parents after a Miscarriage or Stillbirth, the Novena to Saints Anne and Joachim, the Rite of Blessing of a Child in the Womb, and the Order for the Blessing of Parents before Childbirth.

Your Rights during a Loss
(Excerpt from *Made for This: The Catholic Mom's Guide to Birth* by Mary Haseltine)[14]

We believe that a unique human person is created at conception, as science shows and our faith confirms. So the death of that person, no matter how early, should be treated as such. Whether the loss is your own or that of someone close to you, being a people who value every human life means that when it comes to miscarriage, we need to respond accordingly. Mothers have the right to evidence-based care that respects their dignity, as well as that of their child, not only in birth but also in miscarriage and stillbirth.

Regrettably, this is not always the case. In the midst of shock, fear, grief, and ignorance, a mother suffering a miscarriage can get swept into a medical system that may or may not be providing proper individualized attention and care. She often might feel as if she doesn't have a choice in her treatment or course of action, or doesn't receive valid answers to her questions. Because she is in the midst of grief, she may not even think to ask any questions. Rarely are options presented to vulnerable moms so that they can make the choices that are best for them in their circumstances. There are countless mothers and fathers who, looking back on the loss of their baby, wish they had done things differently.

---

14. Mary Haseltine, *Made for This: The Catholic Mom's Guide to Birth* (Huntington, IN: Our Sunday Visitor, 2018), 229-231. Excerpt used with permission from the author.

The following is a list of important points to know when it comes to miscarriage and stillbirth, all of which should be clearly emphasized during a miscarriage.

You have the right …

- to ask to be tested for progesterone levels and receive an immediate prescription for supplements if there is a chance it could save your baby.
- to have another ultrasound to confirm beyond any doubt that your baby has passed before making any decisions.
- to request a copy of an ultrasound picture.
- to opt to deliver the baby's body at home.
- to ask questions.
- to trust your instincts.
- to not have any concerns dismissed.
- to always be treated with respect and dignity, and, at any point, to change providers or ask for a new staff member.
- to know all short-term and long-term risks of a D&C procedure. For some women a D&C may be the best option; however, you deserve to know that it has the risk of causing infertility or compromising a future pregnancy, weakening the cervix, resulting in a future premature birth, or complicating a future birth because of scar tissue.
- to refuse a vaginal exam. If the baby is still alive, it can increase the risk of a membrane rupture and preterm labor, compromising the life of the baby. These exams also carry the risk of infection to the mother.
- to have the father, a doula, and/or another support person present during any medical exams or treatment.
- to call a priest to come pray with you and bless the baby's body.
- to say no to any treatment.
- to choose to do nothing.
- to hold your baby's body and not be rushed.
- to choose some sort of pain relief.
- to have a funeral for your baby.
- to bury your baby. (If the baby's body passes in the hospi-

tal or the remains are removed via a D&C procedure, you have the right to your baby's remains. Be aware that in some states there may be laws governing how his or her body is released.)

- to take personal time from work.
- to name your baby, grieve your baby, and talk (or not talk) about your baby.

Especially when a mother and father are grieving, they deserve to be treated with compassion, have access to evidence-based care, and have their voices heard and respected. Maybe, slowly, as more and more people share their stories, know their options, and demand better care, we can make a difference, not stopping until all mothers and babies receive the care they deserve during this heartbreaking time.

Appendix B

How Parishes Can Support
Grieving Parents

One in four pregnancies ends in miscarriage. If you look around your parish at Sunday Mass, this means that many couples in the pews have suffered such losses. Yet grieving parents often struggle silently, lacking opportunities to speak about their babies as part of their families — let alone part of the family of the Church. Ministries for miscarriage, stillbirth, and infant loss are few and far between. Priests are not always trained to deal with these sensitive losses, and most pro-life ministries focus on abortion. But parishes can live out a powerful witness to the Catholic belief that life begins at conception by supporting parents and remembering their babies in simple ways:

1. Pray for grieving parents throughout the Church year. Include petitions in the Prayers of the Faithful for parents who have suffered the loss of a baby before birth and couples hoping to conceive or adopt. (Appendix C includes a prayer for the Feast of the Presentation of the Lord as an example of how a parish can pray with bereaved parents during or after Mass.)

2. Be mindful of how Mother's Day and Father's Day are celebrated in the parish. Prayers or blessings added to Mass on these Sundays can be unintentionally painful for grieving parents. Consider including a prayer for those who long to be mothers or fathers and those who are suffering from infertility, miscarriage, or the loss of a child.

3. On All Souls' Day remember babies lost to miscarriage and stillbirth by name or as a group in prayers at Mass or in your parish Book of Remembrance.

4. Learn about the Church's Funeral Rites for Children, which

include particular prayers for babies who died before baptism. Consider how to make parishioners aware that these rites are part of your parish's pastoral care ministry. Put together a simple guide for parents in time of need, including steps for planning a funeral Mass, memorial service, or burial for their baby.

5. Create a handout with information on local support groups, diocesan ministries, Catholic counselors, or grief retreats. The less that grieving parents have to search for these resources on their own, the more likely they are to use them.

6. Gather information on local cemeteries, funeral homes, burial options, and financial assistance for grave markers or other funeral expenses for miscarried or stillborn babies. Offering these resources to grieving parents provides practical and pastoral support in the immediate aftermath of loss.

7. Hold an annual prayer service or memorial Mass to remember babies who have died before or after birth, whether recently or years ago. Such memorials are often held by dioceses or parishes during October (Respect Life Month and Pregnancy and Infant Loss Awareness Month) or November, the traditional month to pray for the dead. (See Appendix C for sample prayers for a "Mass of God's Children.")

8. Include hospital or home visits to women who have suffered miscarriage, stillbirth, or infant loss as part of your parish's pastoral care or Stephen Ministries.

9. Create a memorial garden or statue on the parish grounds for babies who have died. Especially for parents who do not have a gravesite to visit for their child, this physical spot of remembrance can become holy ground.

10. Start a ministry of care packages for couples suffering from miscarriage, stillbirth, or infant loss. The parish moms' group could organize a meal train for the family. Your pastor can share the names of other families in the parish who have experienced loss and would be willing to reach out. Possible items for a care package or basket include:

- prayer shawl or blanket
- cross, candle, or rosary

- saint prayer cards
- small keepsake to remember their child
- journal or book about grief
- coloring book or book for siblings
- gift card to a local restaurant or grocery store

APPENDIX C

Prayers and Rites

ORDER FOR THE BLESSING OF PARENTS AFTER A MISCARRIAGE[15]

INTRODUCTION

In times of death and grief, the Christian turns to the Lord for consolation and strength. This is especially true when a child dies before birth. This blessing is provided to assist the parents in their grief and console them with the blessing of God....

ORDER OF BLESSING

INTRODUCTORY RITES

When the community has gathered, a suitable song may be sung. The minister says:

In the name of the Father, and of the Son, and of the Holy Spirit.
All make the sign of the cross and reply:
Amen.

A lay minister greets those present in the following words:

Let us praise the Father of mercies, the God of all consolation.
Blessed be God for ever.
R/. Blessed be God for ever.

In the following or similar words, the leader prepares those present for the blessing.

---

15. These are the rubrics for a lay minister. From the *Book of Blessings*, © 1988, United States Conference of Catholic Bishops, Washington, D.C. Available online at http://www.usccb.org/prayer-and-worship/bereavement-and-funerals/blessing-of-parents-after-a-miscarriage-or-stillbirth.cfm.

For those who trust in God,
in the pain of sorrow there is consolation,
in the face of despair there is hope,
in the midst of death there is life.

N. and N., as we mourn the death of your child we place our-selves in the hands of God and ask for strength, for healing, and for love.

READING OF THE WORD OF GOD

A reader, another person present, or the minister reads a text of sacred Scripture.

Brothers and sisters, listen to the words of the book of Lamentations:

3:17–26

Hope in the Lord

My soul is deprived of peace,
I have forgotten what happiness is;
I tell myself my future is lost,
all that I hope for from the Lord.
The thought of my homeless poverty
is wormwood and gall;
Remembering it over and over
leaves my soul downcast within me.
But I will call this to mind,
as my reason to have hope:
The favors of the LORD are not exhausted,
his mercies are not spent;
They are renewed each morning,
so great is his faithfulness.
My portion is the LORD, says my soul;
therefore I will hope in him.
Good is the LORD to one who waits for him,
to the soul that seeks him;
It is good to hope in silence
for the saving help of the LORD.

Or:

Isaiah 49:8–13 — *In a time of favor I answer you, on the day of salvation I help you.*
Romans 8:18–27 — *In hope we were saved.*
Romans 8:26–31 — *If God is for us, who can be against us?*
Colossians 1:9–12 — *We have been praying for you unceasingly.*
Hebrews 5:7–10 — *Christ intercedes for us.*
Luke 22:39–46 — *Agony in the garden.*

As circumstances suggest, one of the following responsorial psalms may be sung, or some other suitable song.
R/. To you, O Lord, I lift up my soul.

Psalm 25

Your ways, O Lord, make known to me;
teach me your paths,
Guide me in your truth and teach me,
for you are God my savior,
and for you I will wait all the day. *R/.*

Remember that your compassion, O Lord,
and your kindness are from of old.
The sins of my youth and my frailties remember not;
in your kindness remember me
because of your goodness, O Lord. *R/.*

Look toward me, and have pity on me,
for I am alone and afflicted.
Relieve the troubles of my heart,
and bring me out of my distress. *R/.*

Preserve my life, and rescue me;
let me not be put to shame, for I take refuge in you.
Let integrity and uprightness preserve me,
because I wait for you, O Lord. *R/.*

Psalm 143:1, 5–6, 8, 10

R/. (v. 1) O Lord, hear my prayer.

As circumstances suggest, the minister may give those present a brief explanation of the biblical text, so that they may understand through faith the meaning of the celebration.

INTERCESSIONS

The intercessions are then said. The minister introduces them and an assisting minister or one of those present announces the intentions. From the following those best suited to the occasion may be used or adapted, or other intentions that apply to the particular circumstances may be composed.

The minister says:
Let us pray to God who throughout the ages has heard the cries of parents.
R/. Lord, hear our prayer.
Assisting minister:
For N. and N., who know the pain of grief, that they may be comforted, we pray. R/.
Assisting minister:
For this family, that it may find new hope in the midst of suffering, we pray. R/.
Assisting minister:
For these parents, that they may learn from the example of Mary, who grieved by the cross of her Son, we pray. R/.
Assisting minister:
For all who have suffered the loss of a child, that Christ may be their support, we pray. R/.

After the intercessions, the minister, in the following or similar words, invites all present to sing or say the Lord's Prayer.
Let us pray to the God of consolation and hope, as Christ has taught us:
All:
Our Father …

PRAYER OF BLESSING

*A minister who is a priest or deacon says the prayer of blessing with
hands outstretched over the parents; a lay minister says the
prayer with hands joined.*

Compassionate God,
soothe the hearts of N. and N.,
and grant that through the prayers of Mary,
who grieved by the cross of her Son,
you may enlighten their faith,
give hope to their hearts,
and peace to their lives.

Lord,
grant mercy to all the members of this family
and comfort them with the hope
that one day we will all live with you,
with your Son Jesus Christ, and the Holy Spirit,
for ever and ever.
R/. Amen.

Or:

Lord,
God of all creation,
we bless and thank you for your tender care.
Receive this life you created in love
and comfort your faithful people in their time of loss
with the assurance of your unfailing mercy.

We ask this through Christ our Lord.
R/. Amen.

CONCLUDING RITE

*A lay minister concludes the rite by signing himself or herself with
the sign of the cross and saying:*
May God give us peace in our sorrow,

consolation in our grief,
and strength to accept his will in all things
R/. Amen.

It is preferable to end the celebration with a suitable song.

EXAMPLES OF PRAYERS FROM THE ORDER OF CHRISTIAN FUNERALS

Concluding Prayer of Vigil for a Deceased Child[16]

Lord Jesus,
whose Mother stood grieving at the foot of the cross,
look kindly on these parents
who have suffered the loss of their child *[N.]*.
Listen to the prayers of Mary on their behalf,
that their faith may be strong like hers
and find its promised reward,
for you live for ever and ever.
R/. Amen.

Opening Prayer for Funeral Mass[17]

O Lord, whose ways are beyond understanding,
listen to the prayers of your faithful people:
that those weighed down by grief at the loss of this [little] child
may find reassurance in your infinite goodness.

We ask this through our Lord Jesus Christ, your Son,
who lives and reigns with you and the Holy Spirit,
one God, for ever and ever.
R/. Amen.

Prayer of Commendation for Funeral Mass[18]

You are the author and sustainer of our lives, O God,
you are our final home.

---

16. *Order of Christian Funerals*, no. 262 B (A child who died before baptism). Excerpts from the English translation of *Order of Christian Funerals* ©1985, 1989, International Commission on English in the Liturgy Corporation. All rights reserved.

17. *Order of Christian Funerals*, no. 282 C (A child who died before baptism).

18. *Order of Christian Funerals*, no. 293 B (A child who died before baptism).

We commend to you N., our child.

Trusting in your mercy
and in your all-embracing love,
we pray that you give him/her happiness for ever.

Turn also to us who have suffered this loss.
Strengthen the bonds of this family and our community.
Confirm us in faith, in hope, and in love,
so that we may bear your peace to one another
and one day stand together with all the saints
who praise you for your saving help.

We ask this in the name of your Son,
Jesus Christ, our Lord.
R/. Amen.

INVITATION FROM THE RITE OF COMMITTAL[19]

The life which this child N. received from his/her parents is not destroyed by death. God has taken him/her into eternal life.

As we commit his/her body to the earth/elements, let us comfort each other in our sorrow with the assurance of our faith, that one day we will be reunited with N.

CONCLUDING PRAYER FROM THE RITE OF COMMITTAL[20]

God of mercy,
in the mystery of your wisdom
you have drawn this child [N.] to yourself.
In the midst of our pain and sorrow,
we acknowledge you as Lord of the living and the dead
and we search for our peace in your will.
In these final moments we stand together in prayer,
believing in your compassion and generous love.
Deliver this child [N.] out of death

---

19. *Order of Christian Funerals*, no. 319.
20. *Order of Christian Funerals*, no. 325 C (A child who died before baptism).

and grant him/her a place in your kingdom of peace.

We ask this through Christ our Lord.
R/. Amen.

PRAYER OF COMMENDATION FROM THE RITE OF FINAL COMMENDATION FOR AN INFANT[21]
Tender Shepherd of the flock,
N. now lies cradled in your love.
Soothe the hearts of his/her parents,
bring peace to their lives.
Enlighten their faith
and give hope to their hearts.

Father,
grant mercy to your entire family in this time of suffering.
Comfort us with the hope that this child [N.]
lives with you and your Son Jesus Christ,
and the Holy Spirit,
for ever and ever.
R/. Amen.

MASS OF GOD'S CHILDREN[22]
Dioceses and parishes can offer an annual Memorial Mass for babies who have died before birth. These Masses are often held during October (Respect Life Month and Pregnancy and Infant Loss Awareness Month) or November (the traditional month to pray for the dead).

Parents can hear their children's names read in prayer, light a candle in their honor, and receive a flower or candle to take home. When planning the Mass, consider inviting parents who have lost children to serve as greeters, lectors, gift bearers, cantors, musicians, and extraordinary ministers of holy Communion. In the pro-

---

21. *Order of Christian Funerals,* no. 341.
22. Sample prayers from the Order of Worship for the Mass of God's Children were written by Amy Kuebelbeck and Cathy Clyde for Nativity of Our Lord Catholic Church, St. Paul, Minnesota.

gram, you can honor them by listing their name and their baby's name (e.g., John, father of Maria).

SAMPLE BULLETIN ANNOUNCEMENT:[23]

Have you experienced the death of a baby before or after birth? Would you like to commemorate and honor your child's life in a beautiful, healing Mass? Whether your loss is recent or was years ago, you are warmly invited to attend the annual Mass of God's Children. Parents who have not yet had the opportunity to formally commemorate their child's life are especially encouraged to attend. Grandparents, siblings, other family members, and friends are also welcome. Please come early to write your baby's name in the Book of Life.

OPENING PRAYER

Eternal Father,
hear the cry of parents who mourn the loss of their child.
Still the anguish of their hearts
with a peace beyond all understanding.
Through the intercession of the Blessed Virgin Mary,
mother of all tenderness and our mother,
strengthen their faith in You.
Give them the consolation to believe
that their child is now living in the Lord.
We ask this through Christ our Lord,
who conquered sin and death,
and who lives and reigns with you,
in the unity of the Holy Spirit,
one God, for ever and ever.
Amen.

First Reading — Is 49: 13–16
Responsorial Psalm — "Bless the Lord, my soul, who heals the
*   broken-hearted" (Ps 147)*
Second Reading — 1 Jn 3: 1–2
Gospel — Mk 10: 13–16

---

23. From the Mass of God's Children, held annually since 2004 at Nativity of Our Lord Catholic Church, St. Paul, Minnesota.

PRAYERS OF THE FAITHFUL

For all bereaved families, that they may feel God's faithful love and peaceful presence in their lives.

For all those who support bereaved parents, especially friends and family, that they will have the grace to respond to grief with tenderness, compassion and patience.

For all healthcare providers who care for babies before and after birth, may they be guided by God the Father in all they do.

For those families who will lose a child today, that they may be comforted by all of heaven's angels and saints.

For the intercession of all babies who have gone to heaven before us, may their prayers be our constant support and help.

In grateful thanksgiving for the gift of all children, both living and deceased.

READING OF NAMES/LIGHTING OF CANDLES (after the homily)[24]

You are invited to come forward to speak your child's name and to light your candle from the light of the Easter candle, a symbol of Christ's risen presence and our hope in resurrection. Please then place your candle at the foot of the altar, a symbol of entrusting your little one into the loving hands of God. After the liturgy, please take your candle from the altar with you as a symbol of the continued presence of Christ and your child in your life.

REMEMBERING OUR CHILDREN: PRAYER FOR THE FEAST OF THE PRESENTATION OF THE LORD[25]

The following prayer is an example of compassionate pastoral care at the parish level: to create small, regular opportunities during or after Mass to honor and remember children who have died and the families who mourn them.

Today we celebrate the Presentation of the Lord. This is a day to celebrate the gift of life and the gift of children, but also to take

---

24. From the Mass of God's Children, held annually since 2004 at Nativity of Our Lord Catholic Church, St. Paul, Minnesota.

25. This prayer was shared by Aaron Carpenter, Director of Worship at St. Joseph the Worker Catholic Church in Maple Grove, Minnesota.

time to remember those children who have gone before us. We have lit candles throughout the sanctuary to help us remember, and we offer these prayers:

For the beautiful gift of life ...
For all children ...

God, you sent your Son, as a child, for our sake.
For this we thank you.

REFRAIN: Come my children, come to me and you will know
    the love of the Lord.

For newborn children ...
For those lost in miscarriage ...
For those lost to illness ...

God, you sacrificed your own Son, for our sake.
For this we praise you.

REFRAIN: Come my children, come to me and you will know
    the love of the Lord.

For those who have died at a young age ...
For those lost in accidents ...
For those lost to addictions ...
For all parents and grandparents ...

God, as a parent, you understand the pain and suffering of los-
    ing a child.
For this we find comfort.

REFRAIN: Come my children, come to me and you will know
    the love of the Lord.

Creator God, source of eternal light, fill the hearts of all believers with the light of faith. May your light shine brightly in our lives to illuminate the path before us and to shatter the darkness in our lives. We humbly ask you to take our pain, our suffering, our loss, and lift it from us. Wrap your loving arms around us so we may know your love and compassion. We ask this through Christ our Lord. Amen.

APPENDIX D

Books and Documents

Books

After Miscarriage: A Catholic Woman's Companion to Healing & Hope (Karen Edmisten) gathers perspectives on grief and faith from women who have experienced miscarriage.

An Empty Cradle, A Full Heart: Reflections for Mothers and Fathers after Miscarriage, Stillbirth, or Infant Death (Christine O'Keeffe Lafser) pairs Scripture verses with short reflections from parents who have lost a baby.

Blessed Is the Fruit of Thy Womb: Rosary Reflections on Miscarriage, Stillbirth, and Infant Loss (Heidi Indahl) offers reflections, Scripture, prayers, and journaling questions for each mystery of the Rosary, drawing from the author's experiences of loss.

Made for This: The Catholic Mom's Guide to Birth (Mary Haseltine) includes a helpful and sensitively written chapter on loss, including miscarriage, stillbirth, and pregnancy after loss.

Waiting with Gabriel: A Story of Cherishing a Baby's Brief Life (Amy Kuebelbeck) tells the story of a family who received a heart-breaking prenatal diagnosis for their son and had to navigate life-and-death decisions in preparing for his birth and planning to say goodbye.

Vatican Documents

Congregation for the Doctrine of the Faith, "Instruction *Ad resurgendum cum Christo* regarding the burial of the deceased and the conservation of the ashes in the case of cremation" (2016). Available online at http://www.vatican.va/roman_curia/congregations/cfaith/documents/rc_con_cfaith_doc_20160815_ad-resurgendum-cum -christo_en.html

International Theological Commission, "The Hope of Salvation for Infants Who Die without Being Baptised" (2007). Available online at http://www.vatican.va/roman_curia/congregations/cfaith/cti_documents/rc_con_cfaith_doc_20070419_un-baptised-infants_ en.html

ACKNOWLEDGMENTS

Our litany of gratitude is long and wide. For this we give thanks to God.

For our editor, Mary Beth Baker at Our Sunday Visitor, whose invitation to write this book met with our deep calling to serve other bereaved parents.

For all the couples who shared the stories of their children in this book: Anna and Alex, Megan and Peter, Caroline and Matt, Nancy and Bill, Annie and Dan, Jamie and Billy, MaryRuth and Bob, Molly and Ben, Kateri and Mike, Jenna and Mike, Claire and Jerry, Eileen and Patrick, and Mary and Jaime.

For all who accompanied us on our grief journey through infertility, miscarriage, and infant loss. For our parents, siblings, families, and friends who carried us through the darkest days by love in word and deed. For our pastors and parish community. For the midwives, doctors, nurses, and therapists who cared for us, especially after Maggie and Abby's deaths.

For our children's godparents, our coworkers, and friends from near and far who brought meals, sent cards, texted on anniversaries, and brought flowers to our doorstep. For relatives who shared their own stories of loss and strangers who became friends through grief.

For Jen Olson, whose beautiful photos of Maggie and Abby will forever be a treasure.

For the many professionals who modeled for us compassionate care to grieving couples, including the staff of Faith's Lodge in Danbury, WI, and Annette Klein, R.N., and Deacon Jim Saumweber who led the support groups we attended on pregnancy and infant loss and pregnancy after loss.

For the experts we consulted in the writing of this book, especially Joseph de la Garza, M.D.

For Sheila Reineke and the staff of the Office of Marriage and Family in the Diocese of St. Cloud, MN, who invited us to share our story as a NFP Witness Couple, and for the staff of Twin Cities Engaged Encounter who first invited us to speak about marriage.

For the communities of Saint John's School of Theology and the Collegeville Institute, especially for Kathleen Cahalan who journeyed as mentor and friend through all our losses and Barbara Sutton who first helped Laura to reflect theologically on infertility.

For our online communities of support, including the Blessed is She staff writers and numerous fellow bloggers, especially Nell Alt and Nancy Bandzuch, whose faithful friendship and collaboration on the "Waiting in the Word" study on fertility for Catholic couples helped inspire the approach to this book.

For the readers of Mothering Spirit who shared their own stories of loss over the years and supported Laura's writing on grief from the beginning.

For all our children, who remain our greatest gifts from God — Samuel Jay, Thomas Andrew, Joseph Francis, Margaret Susan, Abigail Kathleen, Benjamin Luke, and our baby we never got to hold. For the hope of that perfect joy when we are all reunited in heaven.

INDEX